L'AMORE FOLLE

THE WILD LOVE PART 1

KIRYOWA IDRISA

Indeed, you persevere from the beginning and how it progresses.

You once picked it up, flipped through its progress, and once again, the preamble never talked about you and your struggles but rather someone else.

This time, nope.

You met me| raised me| accepted my faults| and showed me the right ways to live| you and I are highly connected.

Trust me; this is for you.

You who think fondly of others.

You are a blessing to the world, and I am blessed to have you.

|| You know what || and || You know Why||

Namala Aisha, Naiga Amina, and Ssembuya Musa Kateregga.

Contents

Contents

Preface

Based on a true story.

The desire to show the world this type of setting and its beauty intrigued me to write this beautiful book. L'amore folle is a story based on reality and life in an East African setting. It depicts how "love" and its transition from school life develops into something crazy or serious, which might lead to marriage and settlement. It is not a story of happily forever after and not a story where the villains take over. It is a story of how people's choices matter and how they govern their lives no matter what time passes, hardships, or even trauma they pass through. Since I have passed through this setting as a proud East African, I wanted to share how relationships and love develop crazily in East African settings that have been left to drown.

I want to show the world the proper setting of East African teenage life and a bit of mature life. School life is a time that all East African kids will never forget, majorly in the lower secondary to high school. The characters in the book are fictional, but the story is true and extracted from my experiences. The East African Crazy Love, as a subtitle, shows how things in East Africa worked before the spread of western systems in different behavioral settings. Through writing, I always got a chance to tell many people the stories of my life experiences.

I am a scientist by profession (Biotechnologist) and a writer by mistake because I have no degree in literature. I love writing and sharing my stories with the world. I am a narrator by choice because most people want me to speak to them about different topics about life-based on my experiences with them which may give them the courage and strength to keep moving and fight back. My study of science led me to understand that all experiences are pieces of codes encrypted through our life which we must decipher. Writing is just a tool by which we reflect, observe and understand our experiences to make us plan and learn from our mistakes to avoid future mistakes.

The passion I developed throughout my life with the basic knowledge of literature I obtained in my 10th standard and the different experiences I passed through create a massive universe of stories that need to be heard and known to the world. I wrote **L'amore folle** to show the world the beauty and strength of love and morals. The story might be a crazy one, and the shade of the picture might be the ones no one wants to see, but the moral of the chapters gives it its value and lessons to learn.

Acknowledgements

From the true story that brings experiences to putting them down on paper, writing a book is not easy. It is actually harder than I ever imagined. All this piece of work and other works similar to this would not have been possible without the help of my professors, Dr. A. Namani and Dr. P. Eeka, who were the first professors I met when I came to India for my higher education in Gitam Deemed to be University. They stood by me and encouraged me to always keep going forward and keep hunting for opportunities, as well as to keep sharing the mysteries of my journies and their experiences through writing. To me, these were more than mentors; they are my friends.

I am so grateful to my mother, N. Aisha, and N. Amina, who have always made extra efforts and love to support my work, encourage me, immerse me in the pill of love, and give me a sense of belonging. They taught me so much and stood for me where no one could stand. Through these moments I had with them, some pieces of my work arose. Discipline, love, manners, respect, support, and much more have made me reach further than I could imagine. I truly have no idea where I would be if, above all, their parents, Mr. and Mrs. Kapera Sualiman, never nurtured me, for thy I owe them a greater debt.

To GITAM Deemed to be University India, which through the government of India under the merit scholarship, took me in, nurtured me academically, and gave me a chance to be a good leader without looking at my age, and race. My aggressiveness to knowledge and curiosity, coupled with my charismatic nature, helped me grow both as a scientist and a good writer for success in life. This magnificent institution never stopped. Instead, it encouraged me. "Thank you."

Filled with doubts and rage, my life was integrated with ups and downs, but the time I spent with M.J. Philip, K. Abubaker, K. Tarun, T. Solomon, E. Elizabeth, and M. Umar was worth it. This advanced my experiences with people, helped me understand how reality looks and filled me with joy and pleasure. Most of my stories and narrations are pillared on these moments.

Writing a book about the story that existed in part of your life is a surreal process. I am forever indebted to the institutions (Entebbe Parents' S.S and Bulo Parents' S.S), friends from different colleges in Uganda who narrated to me their experiences, and my friends whose names I will not disclose but their stories gave the book its theme and plots. I also further thank you for your editorial help, keen insight, and ongoing support in bringing my book to life. Their guide in the flow, scenes, and connection of the parts helped me to organize and compile this book chronologically.

To the family of Mr. Ssembuya: for always checking up on me (Your son), which kept me moving and motivated. My sister, N. Amina, and my brother N. Shuraim thank you for always letting me know that you have nothing but great memories of me.

Finally, to all those who have added a brick towards the completion of this book:

Prologue

[**Scene**][*A convoy of cars heads to the residence of Mr. and Mrs. Kyanja, natives in the country, and the husband is a former army official (retired commanding officer), where the introduction ceremony of Shantel and Kajjo was held. Honing is heard from a few meters away from the venue as the family, friends, and well-wishers of Kajjo enter the Lujjo sub-county, cut banana plants alongside the road with red, blue, and green ribbons tired around the; Luze the direction to the venue. The wet, muddy road and children running beside the convoy welcome them to the venue with high pitch noise and trumpets from vuvuzelas as the convoy enters the main gate of the family. Kajjo arrives in his most beautiful suit at the Kwanjula (a traditional ceremony in Uganda when the girl child invites the fiancee to her parent's home). Colleagues from his workplace wave behind him, white napkins, and the groom boast as he gets to the main tent entrance. Welcome, my dearest son-in-law, the Mc utters; "we were about to presume that you won't reach as the time agreed upon was due," By tradition, the girl children in the family are supposed to inspect the guests who arrive in the home, this is the first form of greeting and confirming that the primary guest "Bride groom" has come along with the guests. The Mc from the groom's side says, "we had been through baptism and purification ceremonies before coming here. That was the reason for the early morning downpour, so the priest who headed the ceremonies delayed us, which took our time; we are very sorry." "Okay, traveler, there is no harm in coming later, but the harm is in not coming," the Mc said.*]

Had it not been the early morning pour, they would have arrived by mid-day, the Mc continued to speak. From the groom's side, we were all smart, silent, and heavily loaded with different offertories (bride price offerings). Our cultural suits and newly bought shoes made us stand in the mud for over an hour. **"Omutambuze"** (traveler), as the tradition is in our culture, the Mc talked to the leading person of our group and told him to lead the way to the tent, which was built to host the guests from the Groom's side. Had we come in large numbers, the space in the tent was not to be enough. With all the dowery, we were eager and anxiously waiting for the bride. Music plays in the background, and a line of beautiful ladies matches out of the house with the two middle ladies perfectly covered as the bride must be. We all shouted, stood up, and danced, Kajjo in his unique chair, silent and scared. The queue of ladies greeted us in the most beautiful and melodious way; we all responded, and soon was the final moment we were all waiting for. Opening the veil of the first middle lady, we all shouted, "We have come for you; our brother is tired of lonely nights and colds." The Mc at the bride's side ordered the unveiling of the last lady. *{all music suddenly stops in my ears, and I open my eyes widely to confirm what I saw, but it is unbelievable. Her biological sister, Kirabo, had worn the bride's clothes}.*

As everyone was shouting and singing, Kajjo fainted, and we saw him slowly dropping off the chair he was sitting on. All the music stopped, and quickly, people flew from different tents to come nearby the groom and observe what had happened. First aid kits were pulled out, and the function got sabotaged; everything stopped, and no one spoke anything. Kajjo never had parents; hence those who came to his ceremony were friends and well-wishers as he grew up an orphan but hardworking. The old lady of whom she had initially been denied to be in the groom's company due to lack of space in the cars we were using for transportation then stepped out and told them that the lady Kajjo was to marry was not among the two the queue. Everyone then looked in the tent, and amidst Kajjo's fainting, the bride's father also fainted. Marrying the wrong girl is a hard pill to swallow.

ONE

IN THE BEGINNING

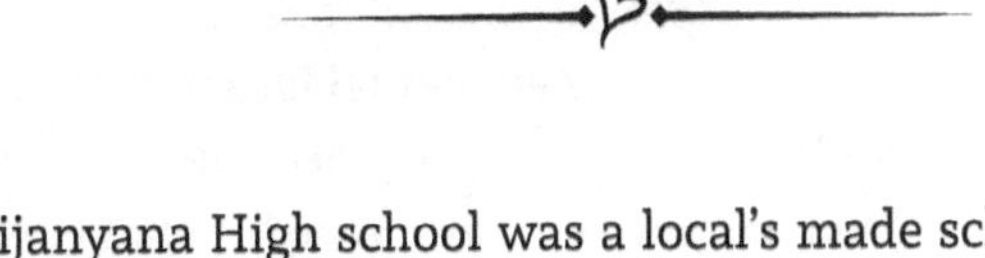

Kijanyana High school was a local's made school that was started to support all the local students in the community who had passed their 7th standard to attain higher education with little expenditure. The school hosted more than 1000 students and had all the required classes till 12th standard. He was built on a religious basis, moral nurturing, and cultural respect. In the course of 2012, he held about 200 students in which; Luze, the son of the mayor of our community, is poorly nurtured and has aggressiveness in his morals. He constantly bullies young boys and disrespects teachers, not even in the top 50 best students in the class. Shantel, the wise girl whose father was in service (Army), is the most brilliant girl, morally behaved and loved by the teachers. She held more than two shirts of "academic giants," a title given to students in the top 5 positions in class for the whole three trimesters. At this time, Kajjo had just arrived at school, and no one knew how he was, whether academically bright or morally well. The agriculture teacher ordered all the students in the class to stand, and well come, the new student. Kajjo was told to stand in front of the class and introduce himself to the class. He spoke only his name and where he came from. When he was asked to talk about his previous studies, he rejected by becoming silent, and Luze mocked him by asking him whether he had raped a girl, and he was dismissed. The teacher then silenced everyone and asked us to welcome him collectively. He was allotted a place to sit and sat next to Shantel, a few students away.

Classes were regular until Midterm exam results were released, and things began to change for Kajjo. He went to the display board to check his name among the top 10 students in each class when he met Shantel face to face. She told him that he could not be on the list; because he was a newcomer. Kajjo then told him he was trying his chances to see; on perusing through the result board, Kajjo's name was at position three while Shantel was at position 2. Shantel angrily went away, and Kajjo followed him. The morning of that next day, on entering the class, Kajjo's name was written in bold chalk, with beautiful, praising words, "Kajjo the new conqueror, the Topper, the Genious and the Great." He felt at home and loved. Luze, on entry to the class that day, reached the board and rubbed off what was written. He then replaced it with abusive and bullying words. Everyone in the class laughed, and Kajjo felt small. Among the people who laughed was Shantel, and this made Kajjo get hurt more. That morning the first lesson was for English, and the teacher entered the class with the examination papers for correction. In our setting, the correction of examination papers occurs after punishing those who performed worse in the exam and awarding those who served extraordinarily. The time was nigh, and the teacher ordered the class captain to read out the names of those who had performed poorly in the exam and were directed to go out of the class and kneel in the pebbled compound. The first person to be read out was Luze, followed by others.

Knees dont bleed

TWO

THE HIGHER, THE HOTTER.

Everyone quickly knelt, fearful faces and sympathy for Dan, who would got two punishments. The pebbled compound was in the middle of the school, making it visible to everyone in the school, and everyone spotted any activity carried out in it. The furious English teacher then received a call from other teachers in the staffroom, "I need support. These students have made it a game to fail English subjects." That was the only message which made sense to everyone. English is an essential subject in the academic curriculum; once it fails, there is no graduation. Surprisingly, Shantel was among the people who failed the English exam, yet Kajjo, the newcomer, passed. "You are fond of failing this subject, yet it determines your graduation from high school. Today we will give you a good lesson such that you always put much effort into English subjects." The head of the English department said. Everyone was shaking, shocked, threatened, and scared of whatever what coming. The teachers had already reached the scene, and they all asked the English teacher whether some people had passed the exam when he said only three people had passing grades, which he mentioned as the newcomer (Kajjo) was among them. "Should we keep getting students from other high schools to come and do your exams? Or should we give you our heads-up during exams? The coupling (boy and girl adolescent relationship) has become rampant, and this is one cause of failure in this class of 2012," said the head of the department of the English language.

[**scene**]*[from the far north of the school, where the staff room is located, one of the teachers comes holding a bundle of sticks around 1.3m in length, smiling he was and even waving at another teacher in another class who, if was interested would join the event. The class of 2012 at Kijanyana High school was all kneeling on the pebbled ground except three people with a passing grades. The teachers, who were five in number, made a conveyer belt, each holding a stick like soldiers on gunfire training, ready to punish. "one by one, you start from my side and go through all the teachers. Each gives you four flogs, and you sit back to class without making any noise." The English teacher for the 2012 class said. Scared everyone was, they feared to start, and some teachers were getting furious till the head of the department raised the number of flogs to eight, and everyone pleaded, "no sir, we are coming." The students said in a collective voice.]*

Luze (whom students had named "Metal" because he was fearless and never cried when punished) was the first to get the punishment. In about 30 minutes, the whole class had been flogged with twenty flogs for poor performance. The next big thing was to award those who performed better in the exam, of which Kajjo was among them. The teacher encouraged Kajjo to keep up the hard work and increase his efforts to be the best, as the world needs the best people. Luze always continued to mock Kajjo. Ever since that day, they became great enemies. Shantel slowly started to join Luze's company, making her perform poorly in the trimesters. The class of 2012 had only one trimester to graduate from high school. Kajjo always tried to help Shantel with academic work, but she never responded positively. News spread over the school as Shantel was having a love relationship with a notorious boy in a school where teachers had spotted Shantel's poor performances and her increased absence from classes. Before informing her parents, the disciplinary committee at Kijanyana High school decided to conduct an intrusive investigation to determine the number of students indulging in coupling and in-disciplinary activities. Luze, Shantel, and other students were top priorities.

After a few weeks of investigation in the school, the teachers had gotten nothing about these incidents. It took about one month to do the end-of-high school education national examination, and preparations were intensive. Students and teachers were all under pressure, revision, and ongoing assignments. One of the days came when Kajjo, who was always leaving school late due to his intensive revision and need to pass highly, saw two people heading to the class next to the one he was in. Later that evening, the disciplinary teacher who could ensure the whole institute was closed with no other person left in any classroom came a few minutes later. "Kajjo, as always, you are the last person to leave the school. I am in a hurry to some important meeting in my community. I am sorry I am to close the school this early today." The teacher said. Kajjo acknowledged and replied that this time he was not the only one who wanted to pass highly through intensive revision; instead, some other people were still in the school. The teacher said he would check out, handed him over the padlock to the class he was in, and ordered him to close it as it had been.

The darkest spot

[scene]

[In the evening, at a dark corner, Kisses and hugs, sweet nothings are said. Luze and Shantel enjoy the love moments in their high school time. The softness of the chain is its strength, they say, but the sweetness of love is its illegal nature. High school love relationships are not allowed in African settings, yet they are the sweetest. "Will you stay in this sub-county after our national examination?" Shantel asked. Luze, who at that time never knew what would happen after his exams, was confused but to keep the love burning, he confirmed that he was to stay. "Don't touch there so much. It's so hot, and I can't handle it." Luze softly whispered in Shantel's ear. Suddenly, as they had just started to boil the pot and the flavor mounting out, the English teacher (Head of the department), who at that time was the school disciplinary master, arrived at the window of the class where the two were.]

"I love you, Luze," Shantel said slowly and pantingly. Luze, whose hand had passed through Shantel's skirt, slowly massaging her thighs softly, said he was to love him no matter what happened. At this moment, the English teacher had just arrived at the class window. Being the evening slightly dark, he could not see them well to observe what they were doing clearly. "Hello, there. Get out and head to my office. You are coupling, yet you read and signed the school rules and regulations. Hurry, up to my office." He ordered them. They both slowly passed through the packed desks and reached the doorway. The teacher then held Shantel by the hand and ordered Luze to close the class. After completing the classroom, Luze ran away and quickly jumped off the green fence. Shantel was left in trouble. Reaching the office, the teacher told her to write a statement of what they were doing in the dark corner of the classroom and with whom she was. After writing the report, she was left to go as the teacher said to handle the situation by tomorrow morning after calling their parents.*[In the darkest spot of the way to Shantel's home (tall woody grass grew beside the gate, a sugar plantation was on the opposite side of the road, and few lights were at the neighboring homes), Luze was waiting for her like a cat waiting for its prey. Frightened and shaking, he was because he never wanted anything to leak to his father, whom he knew was tough. At the far end of the road, Shantel got off the bike, paid, and headed to the small footpath to her home, ambling and drowning in deep thoughts while scrapping her fingernails. Suddenly Luze blooms out of the dark like a lioness grabbing her prey and standing in front of Shantel.]*

THREE

THE NEARER THE BONE?

"Shantel, I am sorry I could not accept being caught by that teacher because he was going to tell my father, and being the mayor, he would have removed the privilege of studying from me, which I do not want. He would send me to the village," Luze pleaded. Shantel looked at him and said she was told to make a statement in which she had written his name. Luze was shocked and angrily shouted at her, "Why would you do such a thing to me? Did you even mean it when you said you love me? Because you have just destroyed my life." Shantel then said that the teacher was to call both their parents in the morning the following day. Luze was terrified and walked away. Shantel reached home, sad and disappointed. Because her father was in service, he was never home on weekdays. Thus, she stayed with her mother and sisters. She never ate dinner that evening, never talked with anyone, and the next day she woke up late and never appeared at school. The English teacher was always the early bird, as he held the keys to the school buildings. He always came early to open them up. In the mid-morning, he goes to the staffroom and narrates to the other fellow teachers what he had witnessed at night. A disciplinary committee was summoned, and Shantel and Luze were called from the classroom, but on reaching the class, none of them had studied that day. The committee decided to call their parents one by one. Before they did, one of the teachers raised a concern that Luze was the mayor's son and everyone in the community knew that the mayor was not a welcoming person when it came to such incidents; thus, he would deprive the child of education and send him to the village which would be bad for the child's future. They all suggested calling Shantel's mother to resolve the issue.

[Ringing phone, quickly the young girl takes it to her mother, "Mommy, Dad is calling on your phone." The young girl said. Shantel's mother quickly picks up the phone and listens, "Hello, we are calling from school, is this Shantel's parent?" "Yes." She says. "Shantel has been involved in some disciplinary cases at school, and we would want to discuss it with her parent before we can decide as a school because she is a finalist, and we would not want to sabotage her study and future." Shantel's mother said, "Okay, I will call her father and ask him to pass at the school. Thank you so much, teacher." With less time wasted, she quickly grabs her money pass and calls her second eldest daughter, who had not attended school that day, to load for her airtime. In a nutshell, the airtime is loaded.]

Shantel's mother quickly called her husband, "Daddy Shan, could you please pass by Shan's school and see what disciplinary matters are there because the teachers just called me a few minutes back, and yesterday she behaved strangely. She never ate dinner, even went to school, minus greeting me. Thank you, dear." After the phone call, she then continued with her work. At the same time, in school, the disciplinary committee was still in debate; some teachers were saying it would not be justice to call only one parent's side others were saying to resolve the issue on one side and leave the other alone. As the barracks to which Shantel's father was deployed was far from the school, it took him about an hour to reach the school. Black army-tinted SUV beeps at the entrance gate of the school. It was break time, and everyone noticed a strange car entering the campus. Four huge, muscular men with army uniforms, red-topped head wears, and black eyeglasses jump out of the SUV; they all match the head teacher's office. At the incident time, all students in the compound froze, and everyone was frightened. In the office of the head teacher, they all entered. "Our boss received a call from her wife informing him to reach his daughter's school as she had disciplinary matters to be solved." The man in the front said. The headteacher then said he had just arrived at the school, and since it was a disciplinary matter, the disciplinary office was to sit in it. Hence, they were the ones who called. He then orders his secretary to take them to the disciplinary committee office, where they will be addressed. "Follow me." She said.

[Secretary walks to the disciplinary office (small central table with three chairs in the back, two large tables arranged side by side, which host six chairs each and a central desk), followed by the four army men. She knocks at the door to the office and enters. The office is half empty, with a few disciplinary teachers seated, taking breakfast. She says, "These parents are here on a disciplinary case of their daughter. The headteacher ordered me to bring them here. I will then go back and do my other duties." The secretary leaves. The four men are asked to sit. They all take off their glasses and army jackets and sit down, following their commanding officer.]

The head of the disciplinary department orders his assistant to call all the teachers on the disciplinary committee. He then addresses the four men in uniforms, "you are welcome, gentlemen. I hope one of you is Shantel's father. I am new here. It's my second year; hence I may not know you as well as you know me. I am the head of the discipline and English department in this school. Your daughter was seen in a perilous action which is not allowed in this school's rules and regulations. So, we decided to call her parents to resolve it." The teachers then enter the office and sit in their respective places. The head of the department went further to inform the parents of Shantel that she had not appeared at school that day. One of the men said, "I am very sorry; I am Shantel's father. My wife told me Shantel came to school today. Could you be more specific about the disciplinary rules she broke?" He then orders one of his men to go outside and make a phone call to her wife, asking her to confirm whether Shantel went to school. The teacher then asked for the statement Shantel had written the day before. "Sir, you can read through this statement as I explain further. Shantel had indulged in the coupling, which led to her poor performance in the previous trimesters.

This alarming scenario made the school survey to know those students involved in this notorious action, and we found many and tried to resolve them. Still, for Shantel and his friend, it was so secretive and highly hidden that we could not find it early; hence yesterday, as I was closing the classes due to the community meeting I had in the early evening, I met them in a dark corner, when Shantel was lovingly sitting on his friend." The teacher said. After reading her daughter's statement, Shantel's father asked who Luze was. Before anyone answered his question, one of his friends he had told to make a confirmation call about her daughter came in and confirmed that her wife said Shantel went out of the home in the early morning wearing a school uniform as usual. He got furious and asked where his daughter was when the teachers told him they could not know her whereabouts as she never entered the school premises and was not in class either. The teacher ordered the gatekeeper to bring the register of the students to confirm, and for the class of 2012, her name was not in the registry for that day. Shantel's father said that even Luze was not in the registry, which meant that the two were together. He then asked who Luze was and requested the teachers also to call his parents such that they could resolve this issue once.

[Shantel's father and his men take action to leave, suddenly, the English teacher approaches Shantel's father and asks him to talk one-on-one for one minute. The two move towards the corridor that heads to the office's exit. Suddenly the bell rings for resuming classes, and in a few minutes, the other teacher rush to their respective class.]

"I request you to help your daughter get off this relationship issue, it's too early, and now her performance is becoming poor due to such unhealthy relationships. The other boy is not a good person, which is why we never called his parents because the only thing that is keeping him not to go to jail and going back to the village is education. So we want him to finish the remaining trimester. As a parent, I ask you to help your daughter." The teacher said. Shantel's father then nodded in reaction to accepting what he had heard then. He then shook hands and ordered his men to leave. Later that evening, the headteacher called for an assembly, and all students were warned against coupling the next time. He then told them that the army men who had come in the morning agreed to help us imprison whoever was found coupling for six months. He then concluded that everyone should spy on each other against coupling and unhealthy relationships because they lead to spreading diseases and death.

Not on the dinner table

[Shantel's father and his men take action to leave, suddenly, the English teacher approaches Shantel's father and asks him to talk one-on-one for one minute. The two move towards the corridor that heads to the office's exit. Suddenly the bell rings for resuming classes, and in a few minutes, the other teacher rush to their respective class.]"I request you to help your daughter get off this relationship issue, it's too early, and now her performance is becoming poor due to such unhealthy relationships. The other boy is not a good person, which is why we never called his parents because the only thing that is keeping him not to go to jail and going back to the village is education. So we want him to finish the remaining trimester. As a parent, I ask you to help your daughter." The teacher said. Shantel's father then nodded in reaction to accepting what he had heard then. He then shook hands and ordered his men to leave. Later that evening, the headteacher called for an assembly, and all students were warned against coupling the next time. He then told them that the army men who had come in the morning agreed to help us imprison whoever was found coupling for six months. He then concluded that everyone should spy on each other against coupling and unhealthy relationships because they lead to spreading diseases and death.

"I request you to help your daughter get off this relationship issue, it's too early, and now her performance is becoming poor due to such unhealthy relationships. The other boy is not a good person, which is why we never called his parents because the only thing that is keeping him not to go to jail and going back to the village is education. So we want him to finish the remaining trimester. As a parent, I ask you to help your daughter." The teacher said. Shantel's father then nodded in reaction to accepting what he had heard then. He then shook hands and ordered his men to leave. Later that evening, the headteacher called for an assembly, and all students were warned against coupling the next time. He then told them that the army men who had come in the morning agreed to help us imprison whoever was found coupling for six months. He then concluded that everyone should spy on each other against coupling and unhealthy relationships because they lead to spreading diseases and death.

[scene] *[Dinner table well arranged (cream leather dinner mat, ceramic clay plates, and beautiful juice glasses with sparkling spoons, forks, and knives. Middle of the table is an artificial flower of roses, and light from the ceiling of the house reflects unto its leaves and wine red flower) children play while shouting in the sitting room. Door knock, "Daddy is back...." The children all shout. Shantel's father was back that weekend. He enters, sits down, and the children remove his army shoes, coat, and bag. With much joy and happiness, the wife comes from the kitchen, "Honey, welcome back, [hugs and pecks], it's been a long week, and we have all missed you. Shower first, and dinner is ready." She says. The husband heads to the shower in the primary bedroom, and Shantel finishes organizing the dinner utensils at the dinner table and heads back to her room.]*

After a while, dinner is served. Shantel and his father cross their eyes at the dinner table as the mother watches them. She then asked what the problem was, and the husband replied that he had yet to get any greeting or word from her beloved daughter. The mother then asked Shantel whether she had studied the last few days because her teachers had called about her disciplinary action. Shantel suddenly stopped eating and went off the dinner table. It was at this time that his father, in a loud, deep, and scary voice, called her, "Shantel, come back and sit down or else you won't ever see that Luze boyfriend of yours when I shoot him and burry him in a place you will never find out." She quickly came back and sat at the table, shaking and frightened. His father asked him to explain her whereabouts in the last few days because she was not going to school but rather disguising herself as if she was going to school when she was leaving home. In a frightened voice, Shantel started talking about her interactions with Luze. Her family listened carefully, and her mother started crying while the father ate his food to completion. He then told her she would take him to Luze's place the following day without fail. He also gave her a last warning about having an affair with Luze as they were still young, and both had to pursue their education first. Then other things could come into play. He further told her never to think of him again, and she will never marry him. Her father told her to go to her room and sleep. The rest will be sorted out the day after. Shantel was in her room, crying all night, and she was cursing her family.

FOUR

THE SPICY THE FOOD?

The following day, early morning Shantel decided to run to Luze and inform him about his father coming to their home such that he should hide. Perhaps she would have sent a text message but did not have a phone at that age. She got up early and padded to the sitting room, making his way to the main entrance.

[toe by toe, Shantel pads through the house to the sitting room to run away from home and rush to his boyfriend's house to alert him that her father was to come into their home to meet his family and talk about their relationship; in the most prominent chair (positioned in the center of the sitting room, more extensive than other chairs, with unique decorations and an army coat, and uniquely hosts the owner of the house), her father sits, organizing his shoes (brushing them to shine and clearing off the dust and debris from their soles and grooves) as he waits for everyone to wake up. Boom, she sees him, and he calls her by name, "Shantel, why are you sneaking in the house? Are you planning something?" he asked.]

She terrifyingly lies to her father that she had woken up to do house chores before they went to Luze's home. Her father agreed, and she went back to her room. Her Heart was beating fast. She knew it was all going to end. Her mother wakes up and starts to prepare her husband's breakfast. At the table, Shantel's mother asked her to tell them more about Luze, and she refused to say anything. Her father was quiet, patient, and soft that morning. After a while, they headed to the mayor's house. Army boots, trousers, and a gun belt with a gun were the first thing sighted by the people in the mayor's compound when Shantel's father got out of the car. "Mayor? You have visitors, dear, and they are army people this time. I think they are from the central government. Hurry up, dear." the wife called in a loud voice. She then allotted a sit to Shantel's father at the house veranda as Shantel was allotted a simple matt. "Welcome, sir. We are glad to have you. The mayor is a little busy in his office, but I have told my daughter to go and call him as this might be an urgent matter. He will be here in a minute. I will prepare something to drink as you wait." The mayor's wife said. Shantel's father then smiled and said that it was okay. They needed nothing to eat or drink as it was morning, and they had just taken breakfast. He then asked the lady whether she had ever seen her daughter before. The lady had not seen her daughter or him before in this community. "Where is Luze?" he asked. Luze, the third eldest son to the mayor, "Luze is inside the house, taking his breakfast. Did he do anything wrong?" the lady asked. At that very moment, the mayor arrived.

[Black suit, shiny brown shoes, in his early 40s; he comes waving his key holder with almost fifteen keys like a dungeon keeper. He then orders his rolling chair (a particular type of

chair that swings as the person wiggles back and forth, majorly made for elders in the culture who were often brought as bride price). As he reaches the veranda, he welcomes the man in uniform and sits in his rolling chair.]

"Welcome, sir. Thank you for the great services to our country. We are grateful for what you people do for us (protecting and defending the country)," the mayor said. Shantel's father accepted the welcome and addressed the issue that had brought him. He told the mayor about his son's affair with his daughter and its effects on her daughter's life. The mayor was so surprised to hear such a thing. Shantel's father mentioned that Luze dragged her daughter into a relationship; hence her daughter's performance at school deteriorated. "Luze ..?, come here if you want to sleep in this house again." The mayor ordered. Luze was nowhere to be seen. The young child came and reported that he had run away from the back door. The mayor had no idea about the relationship Luze had with Shantel. Shantel's father explained that the school had called him once in a meeting, having found Luze and his daughter in love actions in class. "I request you to warn your son and tell him never to see my daughter again because I want her to study and go to the University. Then she can decide whom to marry but not now. I will imprison your son, and never will you see him again. I request you as a parent to guide him well because I am not the person your son should play with." Shantel's father said. The mayor apologized and promised to do as he had said; he also noted that the two parents should work hand in hand to ensure their children won't transgress each other's promises. They all agreed, and Shantel and his dad drove away.

Mayor's wife was surprised to hear that Luze had started a relationship with the daughter of a soldier. The mayor told her wife that Luze was to be taken to the village before he caused any more trouble and turned the mayor's name as he was planning to stand for another term in the community. [scene] [car horns, the gate is opened slowly, and the car is packed. Getting out of the car, he orders his daughter to go into the sitting room and wait for him. Furiously Shantel's father gets to the veranda of the security house and sits, shaking his head. "Tom, come here." He calls the security guard.] Shantel's father called the security guard and gave him new orders to never let Shantel outside that gate unless she was heading to school with the driver or her mother. He then entered the house.

Shantel was sitting on the carpet in the sitting room; his father told him that he was not angry at her and would not do anything to her. He told her that the day she will ever meet Luze, she should make sure that he never knows because the day he will ever know, he will shoot him to death. He further told her to promise that she would never indulge in relationship affairs until marriage. Shantel pledged to his father. Her mother, who was in the kitchen, came in a nutshell. She asked what had happened at Luze's place, and her husband told her everything was sorted, and each family promised their children won't ever meet again so that each family could get peace. She then said, "that will never be true; Shantel nowadays lies, and she will never speak the truth because even the last four days she never went to school, so will she do the final exams at home?" Shantel's father then said he was to watch every move her daughter was to make, and once he found out that they met again, he would fulfill the promise he made to the family.

Sneak like a cat

[scene] *[Luze comes back at night (like a wild cock that does the mating job on the village), peeping like a cat, and rapidly enters the boys' room (four beds arranged in columns of two by two, alongside the walls, the down left bed is his). To his bed, he covers himself with the blanket. A few minutes before he fell asleep, slowly, the blanket was removed from him by his mother, who was waiting for her to come inside. She was the one who had left the door open, pretending to be busy doing more chores outside in the kitchen. She tells him to head to the sitting room. "Mom, Dad is going to punish me severely, and you know how he punishes. Please let me not go there." Luze pleaded. His mother tells him to go and have a talk with his father, and they will sort everything. "Don't make him furious like in the morning of today. He will flog you, and it will be hard to rescue you." She said.]*

His father, "the mayor," was waiting for him. Having paid a glance at his father, his body froze, and his eyes got dry out of tears. "What relationship do you have with the daughter of an army man?" the mayor asked. Luze was dry out of words. He could not speak and started stuttering as his father watched him shiver and shake. He tried to explain how it all started, but nothing he could say to justify his early relationship. "I tried to resist her, but it was challenging that we kept staring at each other. One afternoon in the literature lesson, she approached me and asked why I always kept looking at her. I had no answer but rather to blush away, and I fell out of words. It was the day everything started to strengthen until last when our

English teacher caught us in a dark corner in the evening at school." Luze, in a terrifying way, narrated to his father. Before he could finish the conversation, a loud slap landed on his face. In the same transition to comprehend the first slap, the second had already landed on the opposite side of the face, and furiously his father told him never to see that girl again. He promised him that if he ever saw her again, even for once at school, and the news reached his ears, he would punish him till he could not walk.

Before the mayor could finish his talk, Luze said he would never stop loving the girl. Even if he could not walk, he would have more love for her. Immediately, the mayor stood up and grabbed a rubber pipe to repair the sink, beating him furiously and ruthlessly. The increased voice of Luze crying for his life forced his mother to intervene hurriedly and get hold of the pipe. She begged the husband not to punish his son recklessly. He might cause him to get damages which would cost them much money to treat. The mayor furiously threw away the pipe and angrily said Luze would be sent to the village after finishing his final exams in the coming months. The wife tied to pursue the husband not to make such a quick decision, but the mayor angrily said it was his final decision. Luze's mother picked him up slowly and helped him go to the bedroom. Due to the mayor's order at home, Luze was not given dinner because he had run away from his call during the day.

Pressure on pressure

[scene]*[White shirts, black trousers and skirts, well-ironed, and all the students very smart. "Line up according to your index numbers." The teacher calls. All students rush to the line. Shantel and Luze had been prohibited from interacting. Since the incident at Luze's home, he was not always coming closer to Shantel. "Copying is not allowed, and your exams will be canceled once caught. Please be careful and do not indulge in malpractice." The chief invigilator emphasized. The students enter one by one according to their index number. At the doorstep are two invigilators checking for any suspicious exam malpractice property, all in which the exam started. A few minutes later, Kajjo asks for another booklet, as the voice bounces in other people's ears, "Madam, please avail an extra answer booklet to the student index 091. He has been raising his hand for a long time." The chief invigilator says. All students looked behind Kajjo, whose index was known by everyone.]*

Kajjo, now one of the best in the class, was in the far indexes. Luze and Shantel had opposite indexes (/070 and /007, respectively). In the exam hall, the first paper was done. Some students were caught cheating in exams during the process, and the chief invigilator tore their exam answer sheets. Luze had not studied for long, and based on his facial expressions; the exam took work. Kajjo, who was brilliant, was at the opposite side of Luze's lane in the exam, "Brother, help me? Just slide your answer sheet a little lower I copy only a few numbers." Luze whispered to Kajjo. He slightly slid his answer sheet, and

Luze copied a few numbers. After a few minutes, "Time Up. Pens down and stand up." The invigilators said. The exams lasted about three weeks, and Kajjo helped Luze in almost all the exams.

On the last day of the exam, Shantel approached Luze, and they went to the furthest canteen in the school, Luze told Shantel what happened to him because of her, and he suggested that they should stay away from each other till they were grown up to decide for themselves. Just as they were talking at the canteen, Kajjo, who was passing by to head to the men's room, heard Shantel and Luze speaking, and he listened to their conversation for a while. "We can return to where we used to be at the beach since we finished the exams. I miss the things we used to do there. I want to feel your hugs and the softness of your lips again, Luze," Shantel said in a tiny voice as he touched Luze's mouth. Luze was so overtaken by the moment and agreed. On the other side, Kajjo told the disciplinary teacher that Luze and Shantel were coupling behind the canteen. The teacher hurriedly went to the canteen, and the last thing he saw was Shantel and Luze tress passing through the green fence as he shouted at them to return. Luze then told him he would never get them because his control over them was over. The two ran away and went to Limo beach. Before reaching the coast, they changed from uniforms to casual. They rapidly got a motorcycle and went. The teacher returned to the office and addressed the issue with the disciplinary committee, who, at that time, called the homes of these two students.

FIVE

THE THIRD LAW OF MOTION

**Every action has an equal and opposite
reaction.**

*[Cave curved in the rock at the beach, sunset light strikes
partially in it, creating the darkness and beautiful love scenery.
Kisses and body touch make the scene more romantic; wet
bodies and cold air blows towards them, bringing the evening
coldness, allowing body-to-body connection for increased
warmth. In these romantic moments, Luze and Shantel all
promise to be with each other. It was soon turning to complete
darkness, and Luze suggested they return home when Shantel
covered his mouth and asked him to stay for more minutes.]*

Shantel had been missing Luze and the actions they used
to do every time they came to this place. They used to go
to this place often since they started their relationship.
Because they used to plan their meetings, this time, it was
not intended. Shantel had longed for it, quickly opened
Luze, "I need it again. I don't care whether it's on or not

on. Let's do it for the last time." Shantel said. Luze was so scared of having an intimate activity without a rubber, and he was so afraid of making her pregnant. "Shantel, we can't have sex without a condom, you know. Let's wait next time." He said. Shantel insisted, "it's only once, and it cannot be a bad day; I am in my safe days. We can do it as we used to." After a while, they had to head home. Luze, who at that time was scared, grabbed his bag and left Shantel at the beach. With much anger, shame and fear, she grabbed her belongings and rushed back home. The driver who was to pick Shantel up from school had already reported back to Shantel's mother about her absentia from school after the last examination.

Meanwhile, at Luze's home, her mother was worried and scared as she had received a phone call from the teachers informing her about the incident that had occurred at the last exam with Shantel and Luze. "Mulyaala (local way of calling a wife)? What did Luze do at school again? His teacher just called me to say that we should talk to him. Has he again seen that girl we told not to see?" the mayor asked. She quickly ran into tears, it was unbelievable that the kids were warned, but not even a whole month had passed before they made the same mistake. She then called her husband, and on reaching her, she told him that the only potential solution they had was to take Luze to the village the next day because once the family of the girl filed a case against their child, he would be put to prison and his (the mayor's) reputation would be lost and he might be defeated in the forthcoming elections.

The two parents were deciding what to do when Luze entered and hurried to his room, "Luze, come here. Your father wants to talk to you." Her mother called him. Slowly, he came, muffled, and suddenly sobbed, "What happened?

You can tell me this time we will not fight." His father asked. He told his father what had happened to him during his interaction with Shantel, and the two parents were scared. They asked him many questions and accused him of being reckless and nonresponsible for his life. Mayor, who got so angry at that time, wanted to beat Luze badly, but his wife told him it would not undo the children's actions. At this time, he ordered his wife to ensure that by the following day, Luze was on the next bus to the village. He also added that Luze was never to step foot in the sub-county again. His wife and Luze went away, leaving the furious and broken-hearted mayor in the sitting room. Luze's mother told him to prepare everything that night, and the early morning bus would take him directly to the village.

[Crying and thinking, Shantel's mother is seated in the sitting room, her other kids playing while others are watching television. "God, please protect my daughter and bring her home safely." She prayed. Knocking at the gate, "It's me, Shantel. Please open." The loud, crackling voice of the small gate rushes Shantel's mother outside the main entrance to the house.]

"You are back, thank God. Where had you gone? I have been worried about you." She said. Shantel then lied to her mother that she was with her friends and because it was their last examination, they were having a small party at the end of high school at Joyce's place (Joyce was one of the brightest girls in the class of 2012 who were good friends with Shantel, and she always came to her home for revision and discussion) and her mother agreed. Then she (her mother) asked her about the indiscipline she had made at school that same day, and Shantel never told the truth. Still, she said the party was organized illegally, and she was among the organizers; that was why they called her parents. "Okay, enter and refresh. You will serve us food. Then we can plan for your vacation, as I don't want you to be an idol." Her mother told her. She served the food and claimed not to be feeling well, as she had no appetite. She left the dining table and went to her room. After a while, her mother asked her whether she was feeling okay, and she claimed she was. In the morning, Luze, his next brother, and his mother were at the bus station. "Goodbye, my son, have a nice journey." Her mother said.

Luze was heading to the village, a 12-hour journey in a bus, very far from Kyanja sub-county. When he reached, he promised to call them, and suddenly the bus started the journey. Luze's mother was sad because she knew Luze was not to get the same services and privileges as he was getting from his father anymore. Back home, Shantel had come to check whether Luze was available when she was told the news that he was sent to the village. She was so disappointed and went back to her home. She was never the same for the next month. She could always be sad and never wanted to eat anything. Guilt filled her heart, and her father was deployed to another country where he was to stay for about five months or more. Shantel never talked to her mother as she used to. Every day she developed new changes, and new symptoms began to arise.

[Intensive vomiting with Bleching sound is heard in the main toilet for about five minutes; Shantel's mother comes to check. "Shantel, what happened? Are you sick," she asks. She lied to her mother that she was fine and had food poisoning. She then gets out of the toilet and rushes to her room. She checks her calendar. She gets surprised that she has missed her period. She then asks her mother to help with the money she was to buy sanitary napkins.]

Her mother told her she had bought her some new packs because she knew her month was nearby. She then lied to her as she was using a different brand then, and the older one she (her mother) used to get for her was giving her skin allergies. Her mother directed her to her room at the mirror side, where she got some money and went outside the gate. She was rushing to the nearby health center when she met Joyce. "I was heading to your home; your mother called me and wants you to start studying with me tailoring in this vacation. By the way, where are you going? You look so miserable and rushy. What happened to you?" Joyce asked. She told her she was heading to the pharmacy to buy some sanitary napkins, and she was to meet her inside. She left her as Joyce entered the gate. Shantel reached the health center and asked to have a medical check-up. At that time, the nurse had realized the symptoms (rushy face, pale red eyes, scarlet skin, abnormal blood pressure, and temperature) and called the doctor. The doctor ordered a couple more tests (urine HCG, blood tests, and others).

She was then told to wait outside. Back home, Joyce was given a glass of juice, and Shantel's mother asked her whether Shantel was with any boy during the end-of-examination party. Joyce, among the organizers, never saw or registered Shantel anywhere on the list of attendees, as she told Shantel's mother. Surprisingly, as they were still talking, Shantel returned, scared and broken at this moment, and immediately broke into tears. She then told her mother as she had done the most unfortunate thing in her life. Her mother quickly hugged her and helped her reach the house. She cried till tears made wet her mother's shoulder."It seems the boy I loved never loved me back but instead was using me. He left me at the beach that day and ran away after using me. When I went to see him the next day, he had been rushed to the village, and now I am pregnant and sick." Shantel said. Her mother was highly broken, and the two cried. She asked why she had never told her that she had been having an intimate affair with the boy. Her mother initially thought it was a high school relationship with no sexual activities, so she was not always thinking about it more.

Joyce was trying to ask what had happened when Shantel's mother asked her to leave, and she was to call her again when she needed her. At this moment, Shantel's mother grabbed the results from the health center and discovered that her daughter was pregnant and had other Syphilis. "Mommy, why are you crying, and what happened to sister Shantel?" the young ones asked. Shantel and her mother comforted each other and were to conclude what to do with the situation. Shantel asked her mother never to tell her father because he was to punish her severely, and he had once promised to kill Luze, yet she still loved him. Her mother told her never to speak the boy's name in her presence, and she must find a way to tell her father, or else he would find out in any form or the other. Shantel was so stressed, and a lot was going through her life. Her mother advised her to wait for her father and see what suggestion he would give, but for her as a mother, she would never suggest when someone was carrying another human being inside her womb. The next day, Shantel and her mother went to the clinician to get the best advice and understand the gestation level of the pregnancy.

[Medium-sized lady, brown in color with her beauty, covered with a small veil on her head which clearly shows the structure of the plaited hair style locally called "Pencil." She enters the clinic with her daughter covered with a dull-colored wrapping similar to that of Muslim women except for the eyes. In a white coat, he welcomes them.]

"Welcome, "Maama" Shantel. It has been a long time since you visited my clinic. How are the young children? Is this Shantel? What happened? I hope she worked well for the final exams?" the doctor asked. Shantel's mother was in a saddened mood, she could not answer well all the questions the doctor had asked. "Doctor, I have brought my daughter for a check-up. I hope something is not fine. You can start by seeing through yesterday's tests and then make your own." She requested. The doctor went through all the papers handed to him and called Shantel to an examination room for further analysis. After carrying out other physical tests, the doctor told them that the pregnancy was almost finishing a trimester. Worried Shantel's mother was, she could not hold herself from tearing up.

The doctor, also a family friend, asked them what had happened, and symbolically Shantel looked at her mother in a way that said, "please do not tell him." The mother told him that her daughter had a bad experience, and they were yet to find out who it was. The doctor insisted that the girl file a case so the police could locate the boy before it was too late. Having told the doctor that it was too late, and the boy had already been taken to the village the past few months, he was shocked and could not believe that some random could fall in love with a soldier's daughter and impregnate her and then fly to the village. He then asked the mother of Shantel to decide before it was too late for her husband to know, as he would be furious and make a human hunt on the boy. She could not bear the pain and the challenges her "sweet sixteen" daughter was going through, and the only weapon she had was to weep every time she thought of what was happening. The lady could not believe what was happening in her family, the husband was not coming back ever since he got posted in another country, and her daughter was also going through a challenging situation where she could not make a decision herself and needed her husband to be with her.

How far and how long can you hide?

[scene] *[In the large hut in the compound, the phone rings, and a loud voice shouts from the far, instructing anyone is sitting near the landline to pick it up and know what the towners are saying. Luze, taking a cup of tea and roasted sweet potato, preparing to go to the rice farm for the weeding, holds the phone and calls those on the other side. Her mother's voice calls her by name then she says, "Never think of coming back to town, my son. The man will hunt you, and he will kill you. Rumor has it that you made Shantel pregnant, and now we are all under pressure and scared." Luze's mother sadly speaks and emphasizes to Luze. Stomach cramps go, headache and sweating, continuous shivering, and the bladder gets quickly filled. Number 2 calls in as Luze hears from her mother. "I am dead, mom. I am scared, and it was all Shantel's fault." Luze claims.]*

As Luze was in the village, he had never heard from Shantel since their last meeting at the beach, in the boy's room in the village, he got the news from his mother, and she begged him never to return to town. He was so shocked and could not believe what had happened in just a one-time mistake they made, yet in all the meetings they had, they were cautious and strict. He went to the lake shores that day and swum to the furthest rocks he could see. On reaching, he sat there thinking of many things, which included suicide as well. Luze was never from a wealthy family and being that he was stubborn, it was all because his father was the mayor and he had terrible company. He reflected on how he had destroyed his life, education, and the place he grew up with. He decided to drown himself to death, and as soon as he dipped himself in the lake *[From the far of the rock he was sitting on, fishermen were throwing their nets, and one of them saw a boy dipping himself in the lake. "That boy is going to drown and die. Let's hurry the boat in that direction before it is too late." One of the fishermen argued. The remaining three told him that the boy had swum up to that place, he could swim back again, and maybe he was learning how to do diving. The man who argued with them to help the boy jumped out of the boat and swum to the point where the boy had dipped in the lake. The next thing they saw was a hand requesting help. They drove the boat very fast and reached them. Luze was almost gone, and they had to act very fast and take him to the hospital.]* the next thing he noticed was lying in the hospital bed. From that day, Luze was never the same, psychologically and physically, and even he frequently became sick, tried suicide multiple times, and was utterly insane. *[Heavy car horn, the security guard was asleep, and the young children at home woke him up. The gate opens, and the army-tinted car enters with a red top and army uniform driver. "Mummy ..., Daddy is back. And he has a big new car." The young children call their mother. The door opened, and one of the army men rushed to open the second door for their commanding officer, "Sir, welcome back." The army man says. "Daddy..." hugs and kisses. He lifts his two children and walks towards the main door to the house. "Daddy, Shantel is sick, and she does not recover. Mummy bought us ice cream and bread yesterday. We also saw Shantel vomiting behind the tank. Mummy is always crying in the kitchen while cooking food, and she does not take us to the church anymore," the young children in joy report to their father, who has been months away from home. Shantel's mother comes out of the house, hugs her husband tightly, and bursts into tears as she welcomes him back home. "Please bring all my belonging from the car and take the car for washing. I will call you when I need it." Shantel's Father orders his driver.]* Shantel's father went inside and sat in his chair. His two young children, as usual, took off his shoes and stockings, and he lifted them as they talked about everything. His wife came in with a glass of blended juice, and he requested her to switch on the news. He then took the juice with his young children while watching the news. Shantel, scared and shy, came out of her room to greet her father. At that time, the pregnancy was in the second trimester and had protruded out. She was hiding it by wearing many clothes. On reaching her father's eyes, she was scared to look at him and looked down as she greeted him. "Is this my daughter who used to hug me whenever I came back from long trips? Or she is someone else. Shantel? Can you come and hug me?" he ordered her. Shantel refused, and she just ran away back to her room. He then called her wife and asked her what was happening with her eldest daughter. The wife could not explain and burst into tears again; she requested him to shower, then she was to explain everything after dinner. He was furious, and as he was about to head to Shantel's room, his wife requested him to cool down, as he was just on a long journey and was to sort everything the following day.

SIX

A NEW PLACE TO CALL HOME

During dinner that very night, Shantel never appeared at the table, and his father was so furious and angry then one of the children said that Shantel had never used to eat at the dinner table since she got sick. His father could not bear it and called her down in the sitting room at gunpoint. She entered the sitting room, and he told her to sit down. He then ordered her wife to take the kids to sleep and come back, and he wanted to know everything at that time. Sitting in his eminent chair in the house, he requested his wife to sit in the next chair beside him, "Shantel? I want to know what is happening with you. I want to know everything, and not even a single piece of information must be left out. Are we together my daughter?" he asked. Shantel nodded, and as she started to narrate everything, his father stood up and went closer to her in a furious way; he was about to slap her when her mother held the arm with her two hands. "Honey, she is pregnant. Please do not hurt her. She might have a miscarriage," she begged. He asked whether it was for the boy she was always with or someone else. Shantel never wanted to speak out against the boy because her father had promised to harm him even if he was to run as far as he could. She kept silent; her father was furious, and her wife could not handle the anger this time.

He approached Shantel with a vast force, he held her by the head, and he was about to pound her head on the chair when her mother shouted so loud that it was the same boy, and she begged him not to kill his daughter as children were always in the position to make mistakes. He swore to look for the boy and either beat him to death or shoot him. As Shantel's mother was trying to calm him down, he shouted in a loud voice and said everything was done and he was going to handle everything by himself, and the two failed to control it earlier. The next day, Shantel's father and mother set a course for Luze's home; they went with Shantel because she was the main reason they were going there.

[In his family car, he waits angrily as his daughter and wife prepare to get out of the house. "Daddy, are you also going, or will we stay in the house?" the young ones asked. He told them he was taking their big sister to the hospital, and her mother would join them. In Nigerian attire, her wife comes out of the house's main entrance, and behind her is her daughter wrapping herself in many clothes to hide her five and half month's pregnancy. Sacredly, the two enter the car. His wife sits in front, and their daughter in the back seat. Horn sounds, and the gate opens. He drives away to the mayor's house]

On reaching, the family welcomed them very well and laid down the matter during the process. The mayor's family refused to accept that their son had committed such a sin, and they never agreed on anything. They even called the boy in the village, and he testified that he was not the one who impregnated Shantel. He said that the last time he was with her was when her father came to their home and threatened them. Shantel's father tried to threaten them and promised them death torments, but they were firm in their denial, and he grew angry. The mayor then called the police, and everything escalated. As the mayor was trying to defend his name by talking too much to win the people's hearts because he was to run for the next term campaign in the office elections as mayor, and this action going into public would ruin his image and dower his votes from those who had converged at that time to witness the struggles between the two families.

A hot slap from nowhere landed on his face, and he fainted and rushed to the house. Shantel's father asked whether there was another person who wanted to get a taste of his rage. Amidst all this struggle and exchange of words, Shantel ran away and decided to get lost from his family and the town to start her new life. The news had spread all over the town, and people were all at the mayor's house. People already were having rumors about the army man's daughter who got pregnant by the mayor's son, and they all had to confirm it that day. *[Back to the mayor's home]* The police were trying to maintain peace and wanted to cuff Shantel's father. He went into his car and removed his army badge and gun. Everyone was scared, and the officer in charge approached him slowly and cooled him down. "I will hunt down your son until I get him to pay for what he did to my daughter. We keep fighting for our country in life-and-death situations. This is how the people we fight for to have peace, freedom, and tranquillity pay us back. I will hunt him and kill him because I gave you "mayor's family" the last warning when I was here, and you never took it seriously," Shantel's father furiously said. He left the officer in charge and entered his car, his wife was in a dilemma, and all she was doing was crying. "Shantel? This is the last time I am calling. Come in, and we go home. I am tired of this nonsense," her father shouted. Shantel, who at that time had left the scene an hour back, had reached the main road and boarded a taxi to nowhere. After waiting for her daughter and she was not entering the car, he decided to drive back to his home. Her wife, who was scared and in pain, told him to search for her as she was worried that maybe she might do something to hurt herself, yet she was in vulnerable mode. "She will come back home. Maybe she just wanted to be out of the scene we created back there in fear of getting ashamed, and she left, or even she might have reached home by now." Her husband said.

Fresh start

[scene][*"Nyabo (young lady)? Your amount can not exceed this stop, or else you add more money." The taxi conductor uttered. "I will get off that stop, please," Shantel said. She was utterly a stranger and vulnerable with nowhere to go and no one she knew in this neighboring town. Looking left to right, no one could help, and she decided to walk towards the highway a few minutes from where she off-boarded the taxi. As she walked a few minutes to the highway, taking a small rest at the telephone pole near the wood workshop, Kajjo, working in this place to get money for sustenance and education, was tapped by his friends. "Kajjo...? look, isn't that the bright girl at school, "Shantel?" what is she doing in this town? You were one of the brain boxers who went and talked to her. Maybe she needs help." The friends all mocked him and pushed him. With his ragged clothes sweaty and smelling, he went to see Shantel.]*

"Hello? Shantel?" Kajjo called her from far meters. Shantel was happy to know that someone knew her in the town she had just clogged in. Immediately she slowly dropped down and sat at the roadside. Kajjo hurried and shouted at his friends to come and help him. His friends ran towards him with some water, as she was heavy; the two helped her walk towards their workshop and sat in a shady place for fresh air, and maybe they could have a small conversation to know what she could be looking for in a town she had never been before. Meanwhile, back at Luze's home, the mother, who was weeping for what her son had done which was to cause his death, held the landline again and called back in the village, telling Luze always to be careful with whom he interacts because Shantel's father had vowed to hunt him and kill him. As these were happening, Shantel's family was looking for her, and they could not see her. Luze had the news of his being on the wanted list of dead or alive by an army man. It sparked his mental illness and made him run mad again.

He grabbed a knife and tried to take his life. Luckily people saved his life and took him to the village clinic. As Kajjo sat down with Shantel, she explained why she had run away from home and wanted to start her new life. Kajjo, who was at this time feeling touched by the story Shantel had told her, promised to help her. Being that Kajjo was an orphan and well-mannered, he was always hardworking and loved by his community. He had his small rental just a few meters from where he worked. He led Shantel to his home and offered her accommodation. Kajjo's rental was a three-roomed house, of which the sitting room was the largest, and the remaining two were smaller, so he offered the empty one to Shantel. Back at Shantel's home, the parents looked for her the whole day, and they never found her. Luze was hospitalized due to excess blood loss while trying to commit suicide.

SEVEN

THE BITTERSWEET PAIN

Months passed, and her parents never found where she had run to. His father had used most of the resources to look for his elder daughter, but all was in vain. The police and his army friends all never found her. Her mother, who kept weeping daily and night, blamed his husband for the missing daughter. The husband, who had quit drinking, resumed. Due to this factor, he was no longer unfit for service, so he was posted in the regional army barracks as the supervising officer. Life in this beautiful home never stayed the same, and the regret of their daughter being missing was all on their hearts.

On the other hand, Shantel had started to move on with her seven months of pregnancy and had opened a small coffee and snacks shop deep inside the small town she went to. All through the help of Kajjo, who saved money for the first two months and supported her in starting the business. She also made some profits which she kept for her pregnancy during delivery. After some time, the exam results were back, and Kajjo had passed with a high grade which he qualified to go for a degree in a government institution under the government scheme. Shantel was pleased and sad she could not know whether she had passed and got a chance to get a government scheme. Luckily Kajjo was given a degree program in his town government institution, coupled with an allowance for accommodation and feeding. He was given a degree in engineering which was his dream job. Shantel was about to deliver her child, and money was needed.

[In the town's national hospital, Kajjo, in a rush, brings in Shantel, lifting her with the necessary materials required for delivery. Initial signs of childbirth start as they make their way to the reception. Nurses and midwives are called in a rush, and they quickly hold the moving patient's bed as they get hold of Shantel and place her on the bed. "Hold on tight, mam; you will be fine. We are about to reach the ward," The nurses kept saying. Kajjo, who was currently nervous, shaking, and scared, was asking the doctors at the reception whether she was to be all right. "We need you to fill in this form for your wife, father name, mother name, etc., then hand it over to this nursing sister, and she will let you know where to go next." The senior midwife said.]

Kajjo softly called the nurse as he was not the father to the baby, but rather it was a complicated story which he could not explain, and neither was she his sister, but she was living with her in his own home for quite a long time. The sister told him to fill in his and the lady's names with other details. After that, he was told to pay before Shantel started the procedure. Kajjo, who had never been in this process before, was nervous and scared. "Go into that room. Your wife is waiting for you. She will be taken for delivery in about half an hour after the initial medication is done. You have taken good care of her, and it is hard to find such young girls without infections on their first birth," the midwife said.

As Kajjo entered to see Shantel, she softly rolled her eyes and looked at him, "I am so sorry for having brought all this burden to you. Perhaps things can change. [she slowly raised her hand and asked Kajjo to hold her] I am grateful you are here with me all this time." Shantel said. Dropping tears, Kajjo was out of words, and suddenly the nurses came in and asked him to step aside as the patient was heading for delivery preparations. He was told to bring the materials which were to be used during the process. Kajjo, innocent as he was, never knew what to bring, and on asking the nurses what he was to get, they all laughed at him and mocked him for having made his wife pregnant and during all the time, he never knew what his wife needed and what would be needed during the process.

He felt so hurt, and as he was moving out, Shantel, in a slow voice, requested him to bring the small blue suite case informing him that all that was needed was stored in the suitcase she described. Hurriedly Kajjo went to the reception, where he thought he had left the luggage they came with on reaching, but the luggage was nowhere to be seen.He tried asking at the reception, but no one could give him a clear explanation of what he was asking. Running up and down, he could not find the luggage. Kajjo, in a high state of confusion, went back to the nurse and informed them about the loss of his property. They told him that he was to be more careful as the hospital he was in was a general government hospital, and they were not responsible for the loss and destruction of anyone's property. As he was sitting near the door, confused, one gentleman asked him whether it was his first child with his wife, and he answered that it was and he was not well informed of the process; hence he neglected their luggage, and it got lost.

The man told him that the policy in the hospital allows the cleaners to take solo pieces of luggage to the storeroom, and the only way one was to get the bags out was to pay a small amount to the security person in the storeroom. He asked how he was to do that, and the man headed him to the storekeeper, "Hello, sir. My son lost his luggage as he went inside to see his wife, who is in labor. Could you please help us trace it?" The man whose name we never knew said. The security guard then acknowledged them and told them they were to pay store fees once they found their luggage in the store. He further said to them that the bags left unattended are continuously collected by the cleaners and brought to the store; hence if they found their luggage, they were lucky because most people steal other people's luggage.

Kajjo entered the storeroom and started checking for his luggage, there were many pieces of luggage, and to his surprise, his luggage was isolated in the corner with a wet handle which meant that the cleaners had just entered it. He picked it up and, on his way out, the man he came with asked him to pay around UGX.20000 (8$) to go; otherwise, he had to prove that he was the luggage owner, which was not possible at the moment. With only UGX.50000 (left in his pocket, he paid the amount to the man, and he claimed that he was to talk with the guard to allow them to go because he was to ask them for identification and proof that the luggage picked was theirs. The man then ordered Kajjo to leave and attend to his wife as he was to finalize with the guard.

As Kajjo left, the man and the security guard shared the money, and he went further to get more victims. In a hurry, Kajjo went to the labor room with the blue suitcase;

upon reaching, the nurses were cursing on him due to their ignorance of what had traversed him as he went to pick up the suitcase. At that time, explanations were irrelevant, and he was told to go to the labor word and check for the empty bed and organize it well as his wife was almost going into delivery and the labor pains were intense.

[loud panting is the only beautiful sound heard in this ward. "Keep waiting and hold on tight to the bed. Breathe, push and be strong. You can do it. It's just a few centimeters remaining. Keep pushing, mam," the midwives emphasized. Shantel was in severe pain, and she kept calling her parents.]

As Kajjo was still standing at the doorway to the delivery room, the nurse came and shouted at her, "Useless husbands, we told you to go and prepare the bed in the labor ward for your wife. What are you still doing here? She is about to deliver and will get out in a few minutes. Which bed will she rest at?" Scared he was, he rushed to the labor ward and perused through, searching for an empty bed. As he was still searching, one young lady who had also given birth a few days back called him and directed him to the nearest empty bed. He rushed with the remaining luggage and started preparing the bed.

There comes life.

"Let me help you. Men always do not know how to organize bed and home chores. It seems you love your wife so much. Most men do not come to labor wards when their wives are in labor time. They send their sisters, or even the mother, to the wife always comes. I am happy that you are a responsible husband." The caretaker to the young girl who had given birth said. Kajjo, who had no reply then, acknowledged by nodding his head. After about thirty minutes, the nurse from the doorway uttered, "Mr. Kajjo? your wife has delivered. Could you please pick her up and put her in the ward? We want to use the delivery section for other women as well. Hurry up, please?" He hurried to the delivery room and could not believe his eyes.

[scene][cute baby cries on its mother's chest. Shantel, who was low energy, kept tapping it by the back. "Mr. Kajjo? What happened? Can you please help your wife place the baby in the baby rack, wrap it properly with clean clothes from the suitcase, and drive your wife to the bed you organized earlier? She needs to take good rest." The nurse said. Crying continues, and the nurse quickly grabs the clean sheets of cloth and wraps the baby properly. She hands it to Kajjo and informs him to place it in the baby rack carefully. Shantel is sleeping due to a loss of blood and energy during labor. Kajjo drives Shantel on the sickbed to the ward and slowly lifts her to the bed. "Where is my baby, she slowly whispered as she dropped into sleep, and Kajjo slowly covered her.]

Kajjo, stunned by the newborn's beauty and sweetness, kept looking at it. The caretaker, Mrs. Luba, came near Kajjo and requested to hold the baby. "Kajjo, my son, this baby looks cute. I feel joy and happiness when I see young husbands care for their wives during labor. I pray that God grants the two of you a happy marriage and beautiful children." She spoke. As Kajjo was about to talk about the truth, he was distracted when he heard Shantel whispering, "I need water; I am so thirsty." Mrs. Luba refrained Kajjo from giving Shantel water. She told him the best drink would be warm even though she was thirsty due to the high blood loss during delivery. She also told him to ask the nurses whether she could eat now. Kajjo followed Mrs. Luba's advice and consulted the nurse. The nurse directed him to everything, and things were perfect. After about two days, they were discharged from the hospital with their healthy baby boy. Reaching Kajjo's house, Shantel holding her baby held Kajjo's shoulder and thanked him again for being there for her in all the hard times. Kajjo was also grateful that Shantel was acknowledging her presence. The next day, Kajjo's friends and other people who knew Kajjo and her friend came to his house. They had gifts to congratulate Kajjo and Shantel upon delivering their first baby. Many people in the town were unaware that Shantel and Kajjo were not intimately close, so most ladies commended Shantel on having produced a baby for Kajjo and, more so, a boy. Almost every older lady in town knew that Kajjo was an orphan, and it was an honor for him to have produced himself an heir at such a young age. The problem came when one of the ladies, whom every lady in the village called the senior woman, asked the child's name. Shantel and Kajjo had not even thought of any name.As Shantel was stuttering, Kajjo quickly said that he had named the boy Amos and they were yet to get the clan name. Since Kajjo was an orphan, he could not name the clan's name to his son, and thus the chairman was the person to do it, yet he was not in the station the whole week. The senior woman said it was okay and Amos was a good name, influential and honored. Later that night, Shantel was furious that Kajjo had named her son Amos without her consent. As Kajjo tried to explain, Shantel could not listen, and she furiously said many hurting statements to Kajjo. He decided to leave the house that night and went to his friend's place, where he spent the night. In the morning, Shantel, who was still less energetic, could not do anything for herself and almost got injured while cleaning her baby boy. As Kajjo was still in exile, he received a call from Shantel, and she could not speak well, sounding like she was in bad condition. Kajjo, a few minutes away from his house, boarded a motorcycle and rushed to his house. On reaching, Shantel had fallen on the ground, and the baby was vigorously crying. He got hold of the baby and lifted Shantel to the sofa.

EIGHT

THE SEED OF LOVE.

After a few minutes, Amos was asleep, and Kajjo helped Shantel, most gently, to the washroom. He got hold of the soft sponge and dipped it in warm water, gently passing it over her body and face. Shantel raised his eyes and looked at Kajjo, cleaning her body gently and carefully. She slowly said, "Kajjo? Thank you for rescuing me, and I am very sorry for what happened last night." Kajjo asked her to reserve her energy because she had to be strong enough to walk with him to the bedroom as she was a little heavier. After cleaning her, Kajjo lifted her to the bedroom and rested her next to her baby boy just a few steps away. He went to the kitchen and organized her offal soup and warm milk tea. As Shantel rested in the bed, she kept imagining the touch Kajjo made on her while he was cleaning her, how he was gentle and careful. All this made her get soft in her heart, she clemmed herself for being selfish and ungrateful, and during this time, she cried. Kajjo reached the butcher, and the offal was almost done; he moved to three different butchers and could not find any until he boarded a motorcycle to the nearby shopping center, where offal was sold at high prices because they were processed. After a few minutes, he returned to his house and started preparing.

[Kajjo moves into the bedroom with a tray containing a plate of offal soup, steamed rice, and a vanilla-scented cup of warm coffee. "Wow, that smells nice. I feel like in a grand star hotel today. Thank you. Kajjo, dear." Shantel said. He moves in and rests the tray on the table in the bedroom, "Please make sure to eat everything such that the baby gets what to eat also." Kajjo said. Shantel then laughs and nods her head to accept what Kajjo says. Kajjo exits the door and heads to the sitting room.]

"Dear? From when she started calling me dear. Maybe she likes me." Kajjo is puzzled as he sits in front of the TV and changes the channels with no known agenda. Meanwhile, Shantel was also in the bedroom enjoying the meal, unsure whether she was starting to fall in love with Kajjo or had no option. "He comes home after a night fight, cleans me, and makes me a dish. He has been so nice to me from the day I entered his house and his life. I think I am developing feelings for him." Shantel speaks to her inner woman. Weeks pass by when Kajjo, the excellent husband, keeps making dishes for his sick wife and beloved son. Kajjo was to start his college education in about a month. During this time, Shantel had healed, and she was moving on well with the chores of the house and her small-scale business she had closed due to challenges she had during pregnancy. Kajjo was always hardworking at the workshop, making furniture for the customers, and as he got paid, he could buy the necessities for the house and the baby as well.

Shantel, who showed much care for him at this time, could bring breakfast and lunch to his workplace. "There she comes, the woman of your dreams, Kajjo. God answered your prayer, and now you have a wife and a son. We all adore you." His workmates were always mocking him. It had then become a routine that Shantel could bring the meals and sit with Kajjo and the baby in the reserved area at his workplace and have the meal together as they talked and enjoyed their new life while watching all the steps their child was going through to maturation. After meals, Shantel could always hug Kajjo as she left to return to their home and later to her business. This much care that grew between them instilled a lot in the two, and one of the seeds it watered to develop was the seed of love.

One night as Shantel was holding the baby, it was crying vigorously and loudly, making Kajjo intervene. "Let me hold him, please. Maybe he wants to sleep." Kajjo said. Shantel, in a confused state, brought the baby to Kajjo, who unwrapped all the clothes and the sheets which were coving the baby. Kajjo, who now was shirtless, made the baby rest on his chest with his head next to his neck. Shantel, who had started complaining that the baby was feeling cold witnessed the baby slowly calming down and becoming lively. "Sometimes babies want to feel the warmth from their fathers and the love," Kajjo said. At this moment, the baby slowly started to fall asleep, and after a while, Kajjo brought the baby near to Shantel, who at that time was watching TV. "Hold him. He is now asleep." He spoke. Shantel slowly stood up, and during the transition to holding the baby from Kajjo's body, she looked at him in the eyes and then slowly lowered her eyes to the baby who was at Kajjo's chest. On moving her hands to Kajjo's chest regarding picking the baby, she felt so different and never wanted to let go.

[Shantel picks up the baby and shyly looks at Kajjo, then says, "the baby's body has become so sweaty, and he needs to bathe before sleep, and same as his dad." Kajjo, who at this

moment was bedazzled with how Shantel was behaving, now said he was to bathe. Shantel quickly rushes to the bathroom with warm water from the baby's flask, she bathes the baby, and immediately the baby starts to cry. "Kajjo, your baby wants you again. He is denying me every time I touch him." Shantel said. Kajjo, who was preparing to bathe after, comes into the bathroom and holds the baby.]

Kajjo's entry into the bathroom, wrapping himself with the towel at the lower body, was a spark of fire falling into a field of dry husks. Shantel seemed to have been yarning for a long time for Kajjo's intimate move. As he bathed the baby, Shantel was looking at his body. After, Kajjo handed Shantel the baby and asked her to make the baby get dried, dressed, and put to bed as he finished his bathing as well. Shantel went out of the bathroom, hooked and tortured by the scene in the bathroom. Kajjo, on finishing, went to his room to prepare for the night. Shantel came in, wrapping herself a Leesu (a traditional piece of cloth wrapped by most women, especially during hot seasons and nights, for comfort and easy cooling of the body) and approached Kajjo, held his hand, and closely she held him by the waist. Kajjo drew her close to him and tightly grabbed her by the waist. As Shantel looked straight into his eyes, she closed them and leaped. Kajjo moved his lips closer to her, "Are you sure? You want to do this?" he drawled. Shantel, who at this moment was badly high, kissed him, and the rest of the night judged.

In the morning, Kajjo woke up and was late for work. He first went to the opposite bedroom, where the baby had slept alone. The baby had woken up and kept on playing all by himself. Kajjo called Shantel, "Shantel? Come and see, the baby is playing and awake," he said. Shantel quickly woke up and entered the room. On seeing the baby and

Kajjo playing together, she approached softly and held Kajjo by the back of the head. "Kajjo? Do you feel something for me? I think I am falling in love with you." She said. Kajjo held the baby from the bed and lifted him. He then handed him to Shante and told her he loved her and that what they had between them (as he pointed to the baby) was more than what they never had. "I love you, Shantel." He confirmed.

The day was as usual, Kajjo went to the workshop late, and Shantel opened her business late. As Kajjo reached the workshop, they dropped him a letter. His friends informed him of the letter that the mailman had dropped. The letter from the regional ministry of education told him about the scholarship he was granted, clearly stating the first day he was to go to the college and approve his acceptance for the scholarship and other procedures. Later that night, Kajjo showed the letter to Shantel, who was very happy but then felt sad that she could not know what was happening in her education. Kajjo asked her whether she was having any thoughts of visiting her parents to see whether she was granted government study, and she never wanted to. The week after that, on a Monday morning, Kajjo smartly dressed, Shantel uttered, "Wait, my dear. You not yet smart." She organized his shirt and tie and then hugged him. Kajjo was leaving for his new college, and the good thing was that he was posted as a day student and a nonhostel because the college was just a few minutes from his house.

[At Luumu college of engineering and technology, the freshers sit in a large conference hall. As the college had only a few degree courses, fewer students were always admitted to the government, and Kajjo was among them. The introduction was the first thing on the agenda; each student was to talk a little about themselves. Kajjo is among the last benchers and

introduced himself last. "I am Kajjo, from Kijanyana high school. I have been doing carpentry for the vacation, and I am happy to be in this great college to pursue my future career as an Engineer." He spoke. Applause to him from the Vice-chancellor and others followed. Kajjo was noticed for his bravery as he gave a good introduction and his ambitions in the first interaction.]

Immediately after the orientation, as Kajjo was heading to the office to finalize his sponsorship issues, he met Susan, one of the girls in the class of 2012. "I am so glad to meet you again, Kajjo. It's been a long ever since the time we met at high school. I thought I was the only one posted here from Kijanyana, but I am lucky to have a schoolmate. I hope you are doing fine and everything. Are you in the hostel or?" she asked. Kajjo, who was rushing to the office, talked with her for a few minutes and told her he was not in the hostel because his house was near, and he was glad to meet her in the same college. Upon reaching the office, he was requested to sign the acceptance letters and offer his bank details for which his allowance was to be deposited monthly plus his accommodation fees.

After finishing, he was outside the college when one of the professors called him, "Young man? Come here. You said you are doing carpentry? I want to give you a job. I need a good bed for my house, and I want to trust you with the job because I know you are generous and hardworking. In how many weeks can I get it?" he asked. Kajjo was so stunned by the offer, and he quickly agreed with the task, "In about three weeks, I can make a good bed. Tomorrow I will bring the designs and the types of beds we make so that you can pick one, and we will start immediately. Each design has its price, sir?" Kajjo said. The professor then gave him his contact and directed him to his office, where he was to meet him the following day.

On reaching home, Shantel was waiting. "Welcome back, and the baby was missing you and making much noise almost the whole day. How was the first day at college?" she asked. Kajjo got hold of the baby and went ahead to sit down. He told Shantel about his experience on the first day of college and how he got a job offer from one of his professors. Shantel, happy as she was, got him a glass of juice. Having quenched his thirst, he was served food. A few minutes later, he went to the workshop and informed the boss about the new job he had gotten from the professor of making him a good bed. He also requested him to give him the design book so that he would show it to the professor, who, after selecting the desired design, they were to start making the bed. His boss agreed, and on the evening of that day, he got the design books and packed them in his bag.

That very night, Kajjo told Shantel about Susan, whom she knew, and Shantel requested Kajjo to stay away from her as she wanted to know more about him. Kajjo agreed, and during this time, their love had grown more prominent, and they shared the bed as the child had his small bed, which Kajjo had made for a few weeks. Kajjo was exhausted and slept earlier, and Shantel slept late as the child was disturbed during the night since it was a hot season. At night, Shantel got a nightmare while Luze had come claiming his son, and her parents insisted that she give Luze his child so that she could move on and let the past go to continue with the future and her dreams. She woke up terribly, and Kajjo also woke and comforted her in the process.

NINE

YOU REAP WHAT YOU SOW.

In the morning, Amos was crying. This made Kajjo wake up, and baby seated him for a while as Shantel woke up, and then Kajjo prepared himself to head to college. "Goodbye, dear. Have a good day at college." She said. Kajjo hurried to college, reaching a few minutes late, he entered the hall, and the orientation was still going on. Everyone noticed that he had entered, and the professor who was addressing the students mocked him as he said, "the carpenter has finally arrived." Students laughed, but for Kajjo, it was nothing, as he had passed through a lot worse than mocking.

["Our daughter would also be going to college by now. But the worst part is we even do not know where she is," Shantel's mother lamented. She moves to the sitting room where her husband is sitting, opens the envelope from the ministry of education, and hands it to her husband. "I wonder where you went, my lovely daughter. At least make a call one day. I am sorry if all was my fault, but I need and miss you." He wailed. Children are playing outside, and suddenly, someone knocks at *the gate. "Who is that?" the gateman asks. "I came to see Mr. and Mrs. Kyanja, and I have news for them." The unknown person uttered. The gateman informs Mr. Kyanja, who quickly tells him to allow the person in.]*

"I am, Kilya son to the late Mr. Lunyo. I was studying with your daughter and am also a friend of Luze. I heard that you were looking for her and Luze. Last night Luze's sister informed me that, Luze was summoned to come back to town so that he could get his college letter and start attending college. I thought it wise maybe you could find him and talk to him to see if he could know where Shantel was." He said. Mr. Kyanja, buzzing in the early morning, quickly became sober and thanked the young man for being so generous and having a humanitarian heart. As he reported his news, he requested to leave. Before he left, Mr. Kilya asked to call him once he discovered that Luze had landed in their home. Shantel's father (Mr.Kyanja) promised to traumatize the family of Luze until they told him where his daughter was.

"Hello? can you accompany me somewhere this week? I have a small mission to finish." He said on the phone. Quickly he went to the bedroom and grabbed his army wear and shoes. He spotlessly cleaned and ironed them, polished his boots, and waited for the call. Later that evening, a black army car entered his gate, and four of his army friends came out. "Sir, we are reporting on duty. What is it?" they all said. He told them he was waiting for a call from someone. He led them inside the house, and his wife served them tea. A few minutes, the phone rang, and on picking it up, he said, "I am coming." Then he ordered the driver to take him to the mayor's house.

[Luze has just arrived from the village. Evening tea is served. The mayor, seated in his swinging chair, welcomes his son back

to the city. "Dad, what happened? You no longer have the mayoral office?" Luze asks. Mr. Dungu had lost the mayoral position due to many factors, which included corruption and the rumor that Luze had impregnated Mr. Kyanja's daughter, who at the moment was missing. People had allegations that she had killed herself due to the last scandal where the family of Mr. Dungu denied all the information that was circulating in the community. Mr. Dungu asks his wife to bring him the college sponsorship envelope, which is the main reason for Luze's return to town. "I have secured you a scholarship in one of the good colleges in our country. Go and study. Do not disappoint me, my son," he said. A black army car enters the compound, and the men in uniform quickly jump out. Four of them hold guns while Mr. Kyanja orders them to surround the house as he knocks at the door.]

As Mr. Dungu came out of his house to see the visitors, he had already called the police as one of his daughters had alerted him about the same car which came about a year back had come back and Luze was told to quickly pass in the back of the house and run to the neighbor. "Where is your son? I am going to make him pay for what he did to my life and my family," Mr. Kyanja said. Mr. Dungu quickly denied that his son "Luze" was home and tried to lie for him to be in the village. As he was still speaking, one of the men in uniform came holding him by the belt, "commander, he is here. We can go. He will tell us where your daughter is." The army man said. As Mr. Dungu was trying to beg, they were not listening, and they quickly entered Luze in the car, intending to go.

Before they could go, the police arrived. The DPC requested the men in uniform to handle the case as they were to help. Mr. Kyanja, who never wanted to listen to the DPC, ordered his colleagues to drive, and the DPC stood in front of the car. Mr. Kyanja came out and ordered him to get out of the way, or they would drive over him, and he refused. As he was about to take quick action with a hot slap to the DPC, Mrs. Dungu knelt in front, and the slap almost caught her face, but Mr. Kyanja was a principled man who never hurt women and children. He stopped. As Mrs. Dungu kneeled, she confessed that Luze had impregnated Shantel, but he was not in any plans to make her get lost from her family. Luze was extracted from the army men to the police car and headed to the Police station.

Cases were opened against Luze as he was an adult by that time (18 years). The DPC ordered the family of Luze to get a lawyer while the defense atony handled Shantel's family. The atony requested Shantel's family to meet him in the office the following day with available evidence about the crime Luze was accused of and any other related information. While Mr. Dungu called his lawyer, who helped him in the previous corruption case, he was indicted a few months back, and the lawyer agreed to help him again. The DPC informed the two parties that the trial would be in two weeks, and they were all requested to attend without fail. As the two parties met their law practitioners, they all prepared. The lawyer at the police visited Luze, and he was asked to speak the truth. He agreed to have had sex several times with Shantel, and the last time, they never had safe sex; hence he was not perfectly sure whether it was his pregnancy or someone else's. When asked whether Shantel had other affairs with other boys, he said she did not have anyone else except him.

Shantel's family narrated how they had several meetings with Luze's family informing them to help their child leave the unhealthy relationship with their daughter. Still, the family overlooked it, and when the pregnancy incident arose, the family decided to hide the boy in the village, concealing that he had committed the crime. The father strongly insisted that the boy knew his daughter's location, but he was not interrogated well. He requested to question him, which the lawyer rejected because the boy was a civilian, and yet Mr. Kyanja was an army officer who may call for brutal interrogation; hence the lawyer promised to ask the boy during cross-examination in the court trial. The trial was in a few days.

Most awaited moment

"Do you know that with this crime, you will be sentenced to life imprisonment as it is regarded as rape?" The defense atony said. As Luze got scared, he started crying, and his lawyer reacted, "Order, my lord. My client is being threatened, and he is not in a position to answer the question." The judge ordered the break and requested to have the second witness for cross-examination in the next session after the break. The defense atony and the lawyer of Luze had a small meeting in which they accepted that the boy was guilty of minor consented to sex, "Statutory rape," but kidnapping was falsely accused. However, the two agreed not to make the boy suffer the full punishment of about eight years in prison but serve half a sentence with a fine, as his future would be wasted in prison. In the next session, another witness, "Mr. Kyanja," was called by Luze's lawyer for cross-examination. "Did you threaten to kill Luze because he was dating your daughter?" he asked. Mr. Kyanja got furious and angrily asked the lawyer why he was asked such a question, yet his daughter was missing. When he got angry, the lawyer justified that the family of Mr. Dungu was scared for their son's life and decided to send him to the village till his high school exam results were back. When they were back, they called him back to continue his college education. Mr. Kyanja, furious at the moment, went out of the cross-examination chair and sat by his wife as the defense atony called his last person for cross-examination, "May I call upon Mrs. Dungu for cross-examination." She slowly and sacredly moved to the cell and took an oath.

"Did your son deny that he was having an affair with Shantel? And did you and your husband try to stop this affair?" he asked. Mrs. Dungu, who started crying, accepted that Luze was having an affair, and they tried to make him not continue with it, but all the efforts were in vain as the boy was wild at the moment and was not listening to their advice. She went further to accept that they talked with Shantel's family and tried to do anything in their power; Luze could not hear, and she was sorry to the honorable court for having raised a son who caused society trouble. After everything, the court was adjourned, and the results of the hearing were after two days. At this moment, Amos was making half a year healthy and lively with his parents. Kajjo was almost done with the bed of his professor, and his studies were also moving smoothly. As he came from his last lecture, Susan informed him about the Luze being arrested and in court trials. He asked her what the problem with Luze would be, and Suzan told him that Shantel's family accused him of impregnating Shantel and then ran away from the responsibility. Susan also said to him that the final sentence was to be read in a few days at the court. Kajjo, who never knew the child's father, got to know and kept quiet about it. He continued to move on with his life.

After two days, the court sat for the ruling on the case between Luze's family and Shantel's family. The chief magistrate ordered for the verdict to be read out to the honorable court by the second magistrate, "Based on the evidence given to the honorable court, the kidnapping case is denounced due to lack of evidence and unreliability of the source of information showing that Shantel had been kidnapped, which also never showed any link to Luze and his family. He is therefore charged with statutory rape. He and his mother confirmed that he was having a sexual affair with Shantel, and they both consented to have" sex which they did several times." The court ruled. Shantel's father refused to agree with the court's ruling and wanted to interrogate Luze because he strongly felt that he knew where his daughter was, as the court did not grant his request. "Mr. Luze Dungu is therefore sentenced to three years (three lunar years) in prison for statutory rape with a fine of about four million shillings," the court closed the case. Luze lost it all at this time, and his scholarship was terminated instantly. He was taken to prison to serve his punishment. Shantel's father did not feel that justice was done because he still had a haunting that his daughter was still alive, and she needed his help. Luze's family wept, but as the saying goes, "A criminal always returns to the scene of the crime."

TEN

FAMILY IS NOT JUST IMPORTANT.

Its Everything.

As to what had happened, Kajjo was shocked to hear about Luze's imprisonment. Shantel, who at this time was trying her level best to be a perfect mother for her son "Amos," was that time that the haunt of family craved. Shantel wanted to visit her family for once, and she never wanted them to know when she was to visit because she never informed them when she was running away. Sadly, Kajjo never knew where Shantel lived because he never had a serious relationship with her at school, and only fate brought her into Kajjo's life. One day as Kajjo reached home, he found her collecting the money she had been saving in her piggy bank, "Oh! Dear, what are you doing? I thought the piggy bank money was for the baby's shopping on his birthday when he turns one year old?" he asked. Shantel never wanted to tell him that she was planning to visit her family. "I plan for that since the birthday is about two months." She said. Kajjo added her to the money he had collected for the same purpose.

Later the next day, Shantel went to the taxi station and inquired about the transportation fare to her home place. As she got to know the transport fare, she left her phone number to remind her when she would head to the place she inquired about. During that period, she was always nonsupportive to Kajjo and even sometimes started a fight. Kajjo decided to talk to her about what had happened because she was behaving awkwardly in the previous weeks was pissed by the way she was responding to her and even the things she was doing till when she spouted out the statement of her need to see her family and Kajjo was not letting her go. She claimed that Kajjo was not allowing her to return to her family and never saw her desire to return to her family in her eyes, yet she kept showing it. It was a very awkward situation because Kajjo got confused as he claimed not to have persuaded Shantel to stay with him and never denied her a chance to return to her home. Instead, she never wanted him to know when she was going.

The discussion was long and conclusively; Shantel opened up to him and informed him that she would take his son for his first-year birthday in her parent's home. However, she feared her family might not accept her again after a whole year of running away. Kajjo comforted her and allowed her to go. "Blood is thicker than water," he said. He further told her that she was free to see her family whenever she wanted and never was he in any thought of prohibiting her from seeing her family. Shantel then started planning to travel back to her hometown. The next few weeks towards her leave for her hometown, she was in a dilemma of thoughts in which she never had any idea about how her family was ready to receive her or to reject her.

All these thoughts made her sit on the fence, with doubt about not going but the courage to go due to family and the homesick phenomenon.

[*Foggy morning, with a lot of due in the air. Shantel is awake; in the seating room, she breastfeeds the baby "Amos" while looking to be in a slight depression. Kajjo comes from the bedroom, and as he walks to the bathroom, he sees her seated in deeper thoughts and seems to be in grief and regrets, "I thought you were to start the preparation of your journey early morning such that you don't get late by the transportation program you made earlier?" he asked. Sacredly she turns her head towards him and asks him how he knew about the program she made with the transport people. Kajjo approaches Shantel and slowly sits side to her on the sofa; he gets hold of the baby and pulls her towards his chest, and says, "I heard you on a call with them last two days when they were telling you that the earliest taxi to the place you are heading to will be in the mid-morning." Shantel looks at him, touches his beard, then kisses and tells him that she will miss him the week she is away. "You will always be in my heart; I am just sad that I will be lonely with no tight shoulder to cry on and no one to sleep with in my cold bed. Why don't we go together?" she says. Kajjo slowly helps her stand up and walks her toward the bathroom. "We will go together next time, but you must make it alone this time and establish a good connection with your family." He said.*]

Shantel then slowly started preparations as Kajjo went to his college. During the preparation, Shantel only wanted to pack a few stuff, but because she had a child, she had to pack enough stuff. Kajjo at college was depressed as he would not be with Shantel for the following weeks. "Kajjo, what happened? Today you are not active as you used to be with my lecturers." The professor asked. Kajjo, who at this time could not explain anything, kept silent, and the professor told him that he had scored the highest mark on the test they had done a few weeks back. He was happy, but then his problem was not academic.

"Nyabo? (Local calling for any woman who seems to be old and most especially those with babies and kids) we have been waiting for you. The taxi was about to leave you." The conductor shouted. Shantel had almost reached late at the station because she had to organize the home before she could set off. She arrived late and apologetically requested to board; the conductor mockingly said their taxi was like an airplane. Once the time stipulated for it reaches, they do not wait for anyone; hence Shantel was lucky. Amidst all the challenges she passed through, she was in a taxi taking her back to the town she left in lament of never returning to it. The taxi set off to the main road in about a few minutes, "I have boarded. Please take care and stay safe." She spoke on the phone.

Meanwhile, as Kajjo was done with lectures, Susan observed a change in moods, so she decided to get closer to him, "Kajjo, what is happening? Are you feeling fine?" she asked. He then responded to her as if he was okay. Still, he was having little stress as the people giving him a sense of responsibility and belonging had left his place for another place for a few weeks. He was wondering how he was to live alone in the house and the intensity of boredom he was to face. Susan then got hold of his hand and calmed him down, telling him that things were to be okay, and if he felt anywhere bored, he was free to call her, and she was ready to help him with anything. The good thing was that she was in a hostel, and the college was a few minutes from Kajjo's place.

The two then moved outside the library to the canteen for evening tea. During teatime, Susan talked about the way

Shantel bullied her during lower secondary school, and she claimed her to be a bad friend. She further asked Kajjo whether he knew where she might have been granted the scholarship. Kajjo responded and told her that he was unaware because he was not her friend from school, so he never took the time to find out where she was posted. After the tea, the two walked back to their respective homes (Kajjo boarded a quick motorcycle to his place, and Susan went to her hostel).

[In the evening, the taxi reaches Lujjo sub-county, "Lujjo, Lujjo, Lujjo, send your transport money immediately, and those with smaller notes should help us with change such that we get balance for the rest," the conductor shouts. Shantel and one other passenger get off the taxi, and at the same junction is a motorcycle stage (locally known as Auto) at smaller charges traverse through the sub-country by transporting people to and from the main road. "Nyabo owomwana (Lady with a child), are you going? Or your husband chased you back to your home because you can't fulfill the wife's duties?" they mocked her while giggling. She then raises her hand as a sign to show that she needed boarding one of their transport vessels.]

"Where are you stopping?" he asked. Shantel told him that he was to get off at Mulema's Kiosk, which was just at the sloping path to her home, and the Auto-drive told her as the kiosk was no more, but he was to put her where the kiosk existed before, and it was to be 2$ (8000shillings). She agreed and boarded. During the journey, the Auto-drive talked a lot about what was happening in the town for the past year. "So, you said you were not in the town for the past year? And now, what brings you back?" he asked. Shantel never wanted to talk much about what was bringing her back to town but told him she had brought her son to the village for a minor holiday, and they were to leave in a few weeks.

The Auto-drive told her about the misfortunes that occurred to Mr. Kyanja's family, which lost their eldest daughter as a missing person, and rumor circulated for the past year as the girl had run away to the boyfriend's village to start a life there. He also said that recently the boy the family had thought to have taken the boy in their village came, and he was arrested and put in prison. "You must have been knowing that girl because this place has few people, and anyone knows the prominent families. You mean you never knew Shantel?" he asked. Shantel kept quiet. She said she had never heard of the story he was narrating to him, but instead, she was to stay in the town for a few weeks; hence she never wanted to know what was happening and what happened to the village.

"Okay, Nyabo. We have even reached your destination spot." He said. Shantel went off and clapped her baby on the back. She opened her purse and removed a heavy note of which the Auto-drive claimed to have no change, and he was asking her to board again such that they go to the nearby shop and obtain change, then he was to bring her back to the same spot. Shantel refused, opened her purse again, looked for a smaller note, and luckily, she got it. "Please, take this and keep the change. Thank you." She said. The Auto-drive drove back and wished her to be refined and best of luck.

Home is home

"My baby is back home? Are you sure? Daddy Shantel, you always like playing games, but this time, we will first get dinner before we figure out that riddle," his wife said. The two girls ran to the door and opened it, "Sister..." they all happily jumped at her, and she was so happy. They entered the house, and Shantel's mother, who was in the kitchen, came to see who had come. "Shantel! I can't believe my eyes. You are finally back home. And my grandson, come here, my baby and I am so happy to see you." she said. At that time, her mother was full of beans. No one would clearly describe her happiness; she immediately ran into tears. Shantel was surprised to feel the love from her parents due to her running away. She was not expecting to receive the love she felt. Dinner was served, and her mother bonded quickly with her son, and that night she was the one who fed him. "What is the name of my grandson?" she asked. "Amos," Shantel answered. Her mother then acknowledged the name given to the child; as a religious woman, the name sounded to have a great history in her affiliation. Her father was so happy to have his daughter back, and he told her he tried to look for her everywhere in the town and some nearby towns, but he could not find her. The family was officially reunited. Mr. Kyanja and his wife told their daughter that they were sorry to have been hard on her when she wanted them most, and they requested that she stay with them and never return to where she had run away. Shantel told them she was a little exhausted and wanted to rest, and she was to tell them the main aim of her coming back home the next day.

Her parents agreed, and Mr. Kyanja requested her wife to show their daughter what was once her room, such that she could have a nap in the same place. Her mother led her to her old room while still living with her parents. "We reserved your room the way it was because your father always had a feeling that one day you would come back, and he kept visiting it every week to see if you were back home until one day, he stopped and confirmed that you were never coming back, so he decided to lock it. We are so happy you came back, my daughter." Her mother said while crying and holding her shoulder tightly. Shantel then entered with her son and looked at the room, which blew her into memories. She organized the bed and put her son to sleep. After a while, she went to the bathroom to take a night shower. To her dismay, she heard her parents wondering whether she had come to stay or she was to leave again, and her father mentioned how he was planning on making her stay because she was afraid of losing her daughter again. Quickly she took a shower and went back to her room. Back at Kajjo's house, he was lonely, scared, and wandering in his heart. He tried to cook dinner as he used to when he had never gotten to stay with Shantel, but it was not as expected, tried to watch the television, but all the programs were not engaging as they were when Shantel was around. The house, which was a home, reverted to being a house. No cries of Amos except the smell of him and his napkins all brought much grief to him. Had it not been for the desire for Shantel to go back home, Kajjo never at any one time wanted her to leave. As the nights are seized by day, never will it be night forever, and however much we want things to go as planned, there is always a perfect plan for everything which we always do not know.

The next day, Kajjo reached his morning lecturer late, and the professor was surprised because he had never been late since the lectures started. "Mr. Kajjo? Today you arrived late. What happened? Did you work on your carpentry workshop all night?" he asked. Kajjo tried to pass the question, but the professor continued to tease him as he kept asking more questions until when Kajjo told him that he had a terrible night. There had trouble in the neighborhood, so by the time he slept, it was too late for him to wake up early and prepare for the morning lecture. "Okay, Mr. Kajjo. Sorry for the trouble you had at night. We have been talking about fluid dynamics. Can you please explain anything you know about this topic?" he told him. Kajjo "stayed standing and lowered his bag" explained fluid dynamics, and among the explanations given by other students, his was more elaborate and intelligent. The professor was amused, and immediately after he finished, the professor gave them an assignment and quickly ended the class. "Kajjo, sorry for what happened in your neighborhood at night. I think you should get some more sleep before the next lecture comes in. you can have some rest in my room for the next two hours, then when the lecture starts, I will let you know." Susan said. As he tried to reject her offer, she insisted and told him she had made some good breakfast and was planning to take it after the early morning lesson. She requested him to join her for breakfast, and he agreed because he had not gotten a good breakfast and had a sleepless night. The two sauntered to the campus hostels and entered Susan's room.

Together, we are happier

That same morning, Shantel had woken up too. Grieved and unhappy, she was feeling lonely and not independent anymore. Because she always had trouble with Amos at night, she could always sleep in the early morning, but this time it was different as she was home and not in a place she called her home. "My daughter, may you please bring my grandson to take breakfast? Your father is also at the table. We are waiting for you. Your sisters also need to play with their son," her mother said. She told them she was preparing Amos and would be at the table in a few minutes.

[scene] *[A large circular table, well organized with spoons, cups, and breakfast prepared. A beautiful synthetic rose red flower in the middle glistens. The whole of Mr. Kyanja's family now sits with Shantel's mother seated facing her husband and Shantel just next to his father, followed by Nambi and Kizza seats next to her mother. Mrs. Kyanja requests to hold and feed Amos.]*

"Does he take eggs and milk?" she asked, and Shantel nodded to accept. "My oldest daughter, now a mother, how was your first night again in your family room? I made sure it gets preserved the way you left it. I have been missing you and feeling empty since you left our house." Her father said. She suddenly started tearing up, and her father drew her closer to his shoulder to comfort her and inform her she was strong and she was back home again. He further told her they were ready to support her in anything, and she had no reason to run away again. Shantel then raised her head and told them she would talk to the two of them after breakfast. Her father was eager and told her she was free to speak anything as they were one family. Shantel never agreed because she was to talk to them about sensitive information. Her mother agreed and calmed her down, "Yes, my daughter. We will finish soon, and we will talk about the issue you have in mind. Isn't that okay, Daddy Shantel?" she said. Then Mr. Kyanja agreed, and they had to finish breakfast. "Oh! I had even forgotten that we had removed your high school grades, and last year we obtained a scholarship offer from the government, but since you were not present, we could not avail of it. We will also discuss your return to study if you don't mind." Her father added. Kajjo and Susan had finished taking breakfast. Susan then told him that she was to prepare her laundry as he was free to have a small nap in her bed till the mid-morning lecturer started, and she was to let him wake up once the lecture was about a few minutes to start. Susan then headed to the laundry room and cleaned her clothes while Kajjo took a nap. Before he could drown deep into sleep, he saw Susan wearing short, enticing garments, and she came to her closet to look for the remaining dirty clothes; the closet was located just opposite the bed, and the position Kajjo was sleeping in was so perfect that he could see everything she was doing. She looked for the clothes in the closet and even crouched to see the dirty shoes in the lower section of her closet. This all was so enticing and almost made Kajjo's jaw drop, so he decided to change his head position to the wall and ended up sleeping.

"Yes, daughter, you can tell us what you wanted to inform us about. Your mother and I are eagerly waiting to hear the whole story." Shantel's father said. Shantel looked at both her parents and asked them whether they needed her to be back in their house, yet she ran away with pregnancy and caused them to get disappointment in the sub-county. She also wanted to know whether her parents were angry at her for disappointing them from being a bright girl with a bright education future to a young mother whose kid doesn't know where his father is and whether his father will ever look for him at any one time. She talked to them, and during the talk, her parents burst into tears, and she could not hold to see them crying; hence she also drowned in tears and got lost for words. Her father told her that she was always welcome in his home and would never be cast out because she was the true blood of the Kyanja family. He also confirmed that he would continue searching for her until she got her or her corpse. Her father told her he had tried searching for him for many months, but he firmly believed that if she had not died, she would return to them one day. "My daughter, you are a woman now, and the way I talk to you is more like talking to other mature women because you now have a son "Amos" and this makes you a strong person because many girls who get pregnant decide to abort and the fact that you decided to find your own life that gave you peace and freedom for the past year, I think it is the best thing in life. I am delighted that you never forgot your family and returned to us. Your mother and I wanted to force you to stay forever, but you are now mature and have responsibilities in the other life you have been in. We can't force you to dance to our tune anymore. Just know we are always there for you in everything, and keep us in your heart because we are your family. I love you so much, my daughter and I will always support you." Mr. Kyanja said.

Shantel had tears of love and joy and hugged her father tightly. Mr. Kyanja, who at this moment was being picked up by his drive to the army base, had arrived, and Mr. Kyanja was to leave in a few minutes. "Goodbye, everyone. Let me go to work. I will meet you all in the evening," he said. Shantel stayed with her mother, and they continued to talk. Her mother asked her to narrate to her about her life in the new place she went to and how she was managing because she never had a degree that she was to seek a job, and neither had she ever gone to any other place from the sub-county. Shantel's story is complex and filled with lessons, sorrows, and testimonials. She started to narrate to her mother the story of her new life. "Kajjo, wake up. The lecture will be coming thirty minutes from now. If you feel like taking a shower, you can use my bathroom, and I have an extra towel." Susan said. Kajjo woke up, seemingly fresh, and Susan came close to him, held his hand, and told him first to shower before he could go to the lecture room as his face looked to Muffy like someone from a deep sleep. He agreed and requested bathing equipment and a towel; Susan quickly checked her closet, got hold of a white scented towel, and gave it to him. He tried to claim another towel color, but she insisted and told him to use the white one, claiming all her towels were white. He agreed and went to the bathroom. Susan was so happy, and as Kajjo went inside the bathroom, the next hostel room was Susan's friends, and they knocked at her door. "Suzie, congrats. You got a nice guy; we were told he is bright and cool. We are happy for you. By the way, did he play it rough or soft?" they all uttered. Susan tried to tell them he was just her high schoolmate, but they could not listen to her and claimed she was in love with him. "Don't lie to us; the way you are wearing shows clearly that you two are in a relationship, and how could you just bring a man into your hostel and even change to these types of clothes minus the two of you doing any relationship affairs?" they told her. She was feeling so ashamed and angrily closed the door. At that exact moment, Kajjo finished showering and was wearing his clothes. "Hurry, we will be late for the lecturer." He said. Susan hurriedly went into the bathroom. She then told Kajjo to go as she was to take longer than the desired time. Kajjo agreed, and he left back to the lecture hall. Shantel took more than the agreed time at home, which deteriorated Kajjo's health as he missed her frequently. He had less attendance at classes and work. Life never was the same in the absence of Shantel.

ELEVEN

AS WHITE AS SNOW

[scene]*[On a motorcycle, Susan comes to Kajjo's town looking for him. She asks everyone they pass by to help them locate him. It was her first time coming to this town, so it was hard for her to know where Kajjo lived. Luckily, she contacts a carpenter fellow of Kajjo, and he directs her to Kajjo's home. Quickly, they drive in that direction, and on reaching, she knocks at the door. No one answered, yet the door seemed to be open. "Mam, can you pay me because I have to leave and work on other customers" the biker requested. After paying him, e drove off, and Shantel stayed stranded at the door. In the corner of the house, footsteps pomping their way to the door, "What are you doing here, Susan?" Kajjo is frightened and surprised. "I am sorry, I couldn't withstand you being absent for all this time in classes. I thought something went wrong, so I decided to locate your place and check on you." Susan said. Kajjo gets so socked and requests her to enter inside, as sitting outside would portray a terrible picture to him.]*

When they reached the house, she hugged him and told him she was so scared and worried that he had quit the semester or was sick. "I gave you my number. Why didn't you call me?" she asked. Kajjo told her he had many things on his mind, some of which needed him to rest from classes. He asked her whether she needed a drink or something to eat. Susan was more curious; she asked him whether he was living with someone in the house, and Kajjo told her that he had his girlfriend and they had one child. Susan was so shocked and eager to find out who that lucky girl was, but Kajjo never disclosed her name or showed her any of her pictures.

The place looked so disorganized and filthy that it contained awful ordure. "I can help you clean your home and prepare for you something to eat," she politely requested. Kajjo, who looked so tired and confused, told her everything was fine and that he would do all that. He asked her to return to the university, attend classes, and prevent her scholarship withdrawal. Susan insisted, and she began to do the house chores. She cleaned everything and washed his clothes as well. Kajjo cooked lunch, which they ate that day. After all the tasks were done and lunch was taken, Susan took a shower and, in the process, one of the neighbors saw her and sent a text message to Shantel informing her that his boyfriend had started bringing ladies into her home.

In the evening, Kajjo escorted her back to her hostel, the two seemed happy, and Kajjo seemed to have relief. As he was heading back to his place in the night, he encountered his friends, who seemed to have known about the visiting of Susan. "Kajjo....?, Bro, I have seen you got a new girl after Shantel left. She looks beautiful and seems less troubled. You have to marry that girl coz she seems to be deeply in love with you." His friend said. Kajjo, who felt ashamed and guilty then, called his friend closer and berated him for being inquisitive about everything in his life. He warned and told him to stay silent about what he had seen that day and never tell anyone. He also requested that he keep his nose out of his matters and ignore whatever was happening. "Bro, that was so rude and harsh. But anyway, I will be silent, but remember an eye for an eye. There will never be unpaid debts. Play it wise and cool." He lamented to Kajjo as he quickly crossed the road to his place. Kajjo was so confused and could not understand what next step was to be taken. Knowing where Kajjo was staying, Susan was a big trouble, and this was to cause much anarchy to him and his girlfriend "Shante" together with their baby "Amos."

[Phone rings, and Kajjo quickly removes it from his front pocket, looks at the screen, and it is Shantel, "Dear, I am sorry, but we are to take another extra three days as my parents also plan to come with me and see where I stay and whom I stay with. Is it fine with you?" Shantel says on the phone. Kajjo, who was in shock, expectorated and stuttered, "Yes,…Yes, .. Yes. It is fine. When will you be back then?" He said. Shantel asks whether he is fine, and he stutters that everything is fine. Shantel then tells him they were to come the following week, but the day was unprecedented. Kajjo quickly accepted and wished them a good stay and a beautiful coming back.

"Dear? Have you forgotten something?" Shantel asks. Kajjo then replies that he has remembered everything. Shantel speaks slowly and angrily, "Kajjo, are you sure?" Immediately Kajjo remembers that he had not asked for updates on their child "Amos," and then he asks her how his son was. Shantel exhales and happily replies that Amos is fine and missing his dad too. "Okay, dear. We will arrive next week, and I will inform you before we set off. Goodbye." Shantel ends the call. Kajjo, puzzled, holds up his head and quickly rushes to his place.]

Susan also enjoyed being with Kajjo, and on reaching her hostel, she started planning how to get into Kajjo's life. "He has a home of his own; he is bright and hardworking. What else am I looking for? Me as Susan, that is enough." She said. The next day, Kajjo was working at the workshop. Susan came wearing a spotless white dress looking elegant and sexy, "Hello, I was told Mr. Kajjo works here?" The friends of Kajjo, seated outside the workshop, were so stunned by the elegant lady looking for Kajjo that one of them went inside the workshop, where much loud noise from the sawing machine came. Kajjo was sanding wood for their next project; he was called.

On reaching outside, it was Susan, "Hi, aren't you at college today?" he asked her. Susan then told him that she was looking for him the moment she never saw him in class, yet he promised to attend the following day. Kajjo then told her he was still working on a client's project; thus, he was to start attending the following week. "Kajjo? Don't make us ashamed by speaking with such a beautiful and elegant lady in this dusty, stinky place. Take her across the road and sit down." His colleagues uttered. Kajjo got ashamed and quickly told Susan they would head to the restaurant nearby to have a good talk.

["Susan...? I told you to concentrate on your college work. Why would you risk your scholarship opportunity for someone you don't know back and forth? I know you are beautiful and generous, but I can't allow you to stick your nose into something that will make you lose your college scholarship. I will start studying by next week, do not bother about me." Kajjo said. "I get hurt when I look at your seat in the class, and it's empty. Remember, we are from the same high school, and I am also not free and enjoying with those other colleges because they keep on isolating me. They didn't even allow me to discuss it with them,

and it was you only I am free with. The lectures are useless whenever you are not in class because I am not concentrated at all." Susan replied.]

Reaching the restaurant, Kajjo pulled a chair out for her to sit. The waiter came and asked for their choices; they were given glasses of water. Everyone in the restaurant was looking at Susan. The way she was wearing and the person she was talking to all never made sense and never fitted in the place she was in at that particular time. As everyone in the town knew Kajjo and Shantel, most people were shocked to see Kajjo with another woman of the class above. Susan never minded whatever was happening, but Kajjo further felt insecure. Still, because they had already ordered, he swallowed a bitter pill and continued to talk with Susan. Kajjo, in a very polite and humble way, told Susan that he was so pleased to have a classmate who cared about his education and was always trying his best to attend college classes. He further told her that it was no longer valid to come looking for him in his home or workplace, but instead, she was to give him a phone call which was more ideal and secure for both of them. Susan accepted, and in a short time, the meals were served. Susan felt lively every time she was with Kajjo.

After the meal, Kajjo called the waiter for the POS, and as it was brought, the two argued about paying as Kajjo was to pay, but Susan refused, claiming that she wanted to pay. Kajjo, not in a bad heart, accepted, and when the waiter came to pick up the bill, she got freaked out when the invoice was paid already. Susan asked Kajjo how it was possible, and he told her that in that particular restaurant, he pays monthly; hence the bill is just brought to him as a procedure that every customer is given a POS, but for him, it was a monthly payment. After a while, Kajjo requested

Susan to return to college as he was to finish the work of his customer. "Kajjo, we envy you. All the beautiful ladies come your way. Now look, "all his colleagues pointed at one of their fellows" Kalungi has never had any lady whisper to him, and yet he whispers to many, and they end up abusing him," they all uttered. Kajjo laughed and told them to leave Kalungi alone as he was still a young man who wanted to make good fortune in carpentry.

The turce to remember

[*"Mom? Dad? What time are we starting the journey? I need to tell Kajjo because he is sometimes at college or a workshop, so when I tell him, at least he will make sure to be home by the time we arrive." Shantel asks her parents. Mr. Kyanja tells his driver to warm up the car and prepare for departing. Shantel's mother wearing so beautifully and elegantly, comes out in her turquoise Nigerian attire, followed by her two daughters' cyan and magenta clothing. Her dad finally pops out of the hive in his elegant royal blue Kitenji (Local attire similar to that of Nigerian but different in style), and Shantel with his son comes out last as Amos ambles in his navy blue wearing and sharp cap and Shantel wobbles slowly in her green long majestic dress. They all enter the car. Shantel sits in front of the car with the driver and her son to show them the direction to the place. The gate opens, and the car drives out.]*

"We are setting off now. My family and I are coming, and we are so excited to meet you." Shantel talks with Kajjo on the phone. Kajjo then acknowledges their coming and promises to be home by the time they arrive. He was at the workshop and decided to rush to the restaurant to make a bulk order of around seven people. He requested his friends to help him finish the vanishing part he was working on, as he was hosting important visitors quickly. Kalungi took the task as he was not working on anything.

The phone rings again. He picks it up. "Kajjo, you promised to attend lectures this week, but today "Monday" you did not come? Is there any problem? I want to come and am on my way to your home?" Susan said. Shocked Kajjo, he immediately told Susan not to come to his place because he had visitors from her girlfriend's home and never wanted to have misunderstandings. Susan quickly hung up the phone and left him in a dilemma. Kajjo then quickly went to his place, cleaned it up, and organized it a little. He never knew that Shantel had called some of her fellow women in town and told them that she was coming with her family, so they were welcome to visit her place.

A few minutes after cleaning, Kajjo started to see the senior women in town approaching his home. "Mam? Is there any problem? I have not called anyone from the village to visit?" Kajjo said. One of the women told him that his girlfriend called them and informed them that she was coming back and her family was also visiting the place she resides in and the people she lives in, so she wanted us to meet her parents too. Kajjo then accepted and allowed them to enter the house. On entry, they told him he had made poor organizations in the place, so they all returned to their homes and brought mats and good carpets, which they laid down and organized well. A big Pajero was seen approaching Kajjo's home in a few minutes, and everyone was surprised. [Shantel comes out of the car and immediately hugs the ladies who are around, thanking them for coming. Amos quickly runs to Kajjo "Daddy.." he quickly lifts and pecks him on his cheek. "Mom and Dad, please come and meet my family I met and made here in this town," Shantel said. The driver comes out and quickly rushes to open the third door where Mr. and Mrs. Kyanja are seated. The two daughters quickly open their car doors and rush out, "Sister Shantel? Is this Mr. Kajjo, the father to Amos?" they all ask inquisitively. She told them he was the one, and they all went near him, knelt, and greeted him.

Meanwhile, Mr. and Mrs. Kyanja came out of the car and greeted the people to host them. The senior woman came forward and greeted them further, and requested them to enter the house. They all entered, and Kajjo and Shantel's father sat on the sofa while the rest of the women sat down. A senior woman who was also the wife of the town chairman said that the chairman was to come in a few minutes. The guests were served soda and juice. Shantel introduced her parents, starting with her father, mother, and two sisters. "May I enter, please? I am pleased to welcome our guests to our town; Kajjo is our son. We take honor and respect to welcome you and treat you well in this town as you decided to come and visit a place where your daughter and our son live in harmony," The mayor said. Having sat down in the chair just next to Mr. Kyanja. The senior woman requested her fellow women to serve the visitors lunch as they were from a long journey. Lunch was served, and the conversations continued.

Beyond the outskirts of the Kajjo's home was Susan watching everything. As they all entered the house, she also left angrily. She tried calling Kajjo several times, but his phone was off. As the meeting with Kajjo and Shantel's family continued, Kajjo went out with Amos and the two girls to buy them, sweets. On reaching the shop nearer to his workshop, Kalungi told him that Susan had come looking for him. He was so shocked, and immediately he pulled out his phone and switched it on. He called Susan, but her phone was off. Kajjo was so worried and scared. "Did she come here only, or she reached my home too?" he asked. Kalungi told him, "she only passed here and found me varnishing that furniture you left me with, and the only message she left you was, "please tell him I passed by and he should not call me again. He is a liar." So I just told you." It was the most challenging and painful log Kajjo had ever been hit with because he never knew what to do or what Susan was planning next. After all, right from high school, she was a girl who never stopped until she got what she wanted or destroyed everything. He quickly held the kids and went back to his home. During the talk between the chairman, the senior woman, and Mr. and Mrs. Kyanja, they all agreed that once Kajjo finishes his degree, they should get married to Shantel so that they can be legally married and avoid an unlawful relationship. All these were discussed when Shantel was ordered to head to the nearest coke station and bring more drinks with her friend Nankya, a vendor in this town. Nankya told Shantel about the woman she saw who visited Kajjo once in his home and requested her to be keen on her. She seemed to have bad intentions. When both Kajjo and Shantel returned, they enjoyed the remaining minutes before Mr. and Mrs. Kyanja's family returned. The entire visit was memorable, and Shantel's parents, mostly the mother, cried when she was leaving her daughter again.

Sypnosis

The book La'more folle tells a story of a young couple that went against all odds to fight for love. In the Lujjo sub-county, the story begins when Shantel and Kajjo are at the traditional wedding ceremony. Things fall apart. Shantel runs off the wedding event and goes to fight something much bigger. Shantel, who was the daughter of a wealthy retired army father, Mr. Kyanja, bright as she was, decided to fall in love with Kajjo, the mayor's son at present. This relationship made the two indulge in sexual activities, which caused Shantel to get pregnant early, and both lost their education careers. Shantel ran away from home at a very young age due to the high stress and shame she had caused her parents.

Kajjo, Luze, Shantel, and Susan were students at Kijanyana high school in the class of 2012, all graduated, and most of them got government scholarships for college education. Luze's family knew that their son had impregnated Shantel, and it was to bring disgrace to them, so they hid him in the village with hopes of keeping him away from trouble and their family name. As justice must be served, the day he returned to his home under his father's request, he was arrested and imprisoned for minor rape, making his life miserable. Kajjo, who became a rescue for Shantel, played a significant role in her life as a caretaker and a father to their baby "Amos." Shantel's absence from Kajjo during her visit to her parents after one year of runaway gave room for Susan, Kajjo's college mate, to trap Kajjo and make him dwell in the well of her love. Shantel and Kajjo's love was naturally induced, so Kajjo loved her wholeheartedly. However, Susan tried to make him abandon Shantel, but he could not, which sparked the fight between women making life of Kajjo a living hell. Susan worked toe and nail, making things difficult for Kajjo and Shantel. She even made a sole friendship with Luze during his time in prison, and on his release, Susan became his funder to compose a rebellious truce against Shantel and Kajjo.

During Kajjo's wedding meetings, Susan was among the people whom Kajjo trusted, but she was striking him in the back. She made threatening plans to sabotage the ceremony. Luckily, the ceremony was organized when Kajjo discovered who Susan was in his life and little did he know that she had much bigger plans of destroying his life with Shantel than a mere wedding ceremony. On the day of the ceremony, she abducted Amos with the help of Luze, "Amos's biological father," which was never spotted at the moment but later, when Kajjo and his friends entered the wedding venue, a phone call to Shantel's mother was made claiming for Shantel's action in need to release her son. She was informed to meet them at a specific place she had to go alone. Shantel then decided to leave the wedding ceremony and asked her cousin's sister to disguise herself as her. This tragedy disappointed Kajjo and his friends; Shantel's father collapsed. Strong as she was, Shantel fought for her love, and by the time her mother informed people what had happened so that they could go for her rescue, she was being held and locked up by Luze, who claimed to have loved him so much. The police and crowd made their move and rescued Shantel with her son, and Luze with his evil companion Susan was taken to prison with huge charges. After healing, his father promised to organize a wedding party for her and Kajjo in compensation for the loss Kajjo made in the first wedding. In the white gown and royal blue tuxedo, the two enter the ceremony, Amos and Kizza in the front. The wedding ceremony commences. "Forever, in sickness, in wealth, poverty, and life," they vowed.

You may Kiss the bride.

Author's Biography

Kiryowa Idrisa is a Ugandan National by descent whose parents are Namala Aisha of the Ngabi (antelope) clan and Ssembuya Musa Kateregga, the Mpeewo (Deer) clan. Both are citizens of Uganda under the same scheme and residents of the Wakiso district. Born on 13th April at the peak of the end of the 20th century, in Entebbe grade B hospital, he was raised by his grandparents, Mr. and Mrs. Kapera Sulaiman of Wakiso district in Entebbe Municipality.

His first formal education was at Entebbe Quran Primary school, later transfered to Uganda Air Force Primary school, where he completed his primary level and merged as the best candidate for his class. He then got admitted to Entebbe Secondary School, where his father had studied before. Later he changed to a school where his mother was a teacher "Entebbe's Parents' Secondary school" which nurtured and molded him into what we can see today. With his passion for science, he developed excellent analytical and observational skills. His English teachers, Mr. Bantu Aaron Norris and Mr. Kizito Musa worked tooth and nail to improve his literacy skills. He was the best in his class at national exams.

Pushing to another level of education, he got a bursary to study in one of the best Muslim schools in Uganda, "Bulo Parents Secondary School". He enhanced his leadership skills,religious knowledge and grew his passion for scientific significantly. High credits goes to, Mr. Lwanga Ali and Mr. Lukyamuzi Ali, who enhanced his mathematics skills, and Mr. Kassagga togehther with Mr. Collin who improved his observational and analytical skills. He graduated from high school among the top ten of his class.

in 2019, he dropped his fist college degree at Kisubi University and followed his dream of studying abroad. He was granted admission to the Gandhi institute of technology and management (GITAM, Deemed to be a University) in India. He was admitted for a conjugate bachelor's course in Biotechnology, Chemistry, and Microbiology. He decided to use this step and pathway to develop many skills he had a calling on. While studying at GITAM university, he participated in many international and national activities such as conferences, debates, writing competitions, leadership, and collaborative research with Ph.D. students.

In 2022, he secured a fully funded trip to Egypt to attend the World Youth Forum 2021 as a delegate from India with his start-up. The two weeks trip groomed him through interactions with different world youths and leaders and seeing the other innovative ideas from the youths worldwide. From then, he developed a love for being a sustainable development activist. His visit to Egypt was a significant milestone. It paved the way for developing a science leadership club, "Biotechnology Club GITAM," which helped young scientists grow as leaders, innovators, and researchers for sustainable innovations using available resources. In the same year, due to his exquisite character, he was selected for a student employment opportunity at GITAM to help him subsidize his living and leadership and promote sustainability. He was recruited by the research and constancy department, which helped him obtain working skills and liaise with researchers. The part-time recruitment helped him learn more and opened up more opportunities. In the middle of the year, he secured a fully funded opportunity to Europe under sustainability which enhanced his understanding of sustainability, leadership, culture, and democracy under the Sustain MV program.

Kiryowa Idrisa also takes his bachelor's of health science as a distance learning program at the University of the People (UoPeople) which he opts to merge with his bachelor's to help him in the profession he hopes to seek for. He is a passionate writer whose writing is not based on his work but rather on his experiences throughout his life. He has written several scripts like the Egypt Boy, The journey of 1000 miles, The breath of Europe, and his current book, L'amore folle, and amongst them, only "The breathe of Europe" has been published. He also wrote poems (the dying man's lament) and short stories (the crow of Uganda), which were also not published but helped him win milestones in writing. He was given a silver award, having emerged runner-up in the Queen's commonwealth essay writing competitions. A lot can be said about Mr. Kiryowa Idrisa, but since he is still a growing scientist and writer, his biography still has a lot more to be added.